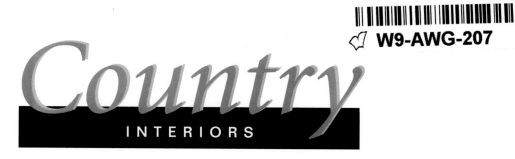

# Country
## INTERIORS

## ROOM *by* ROOM

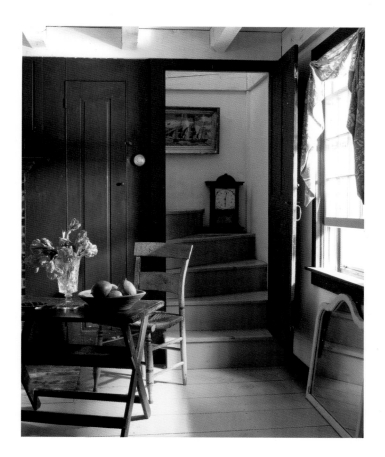

GLOUCESTER MASSACHUSETTS

ROCKPORT PUBLISHERS

## CAROL MEREDITH

First published in the United States of America by
Rockport Publishers, Inc.
33 Commercial Street
Gloucester, Massachusetts  01930-5089
Telephone: (978) 282-9590
Facsimile: (978) 283-2742
www.rockpub.com

ISBN 1-56496-700-X

10 9 8 7 6 5 4 3 2 1

Design: Argus Visual Communication, Boston, Massachusetts
Front cover image: Eric Roth Studio
Back cover photos (clockwise from top right): Eric Roth (credits appear on page 22); Bill Rothschild (credits appear on page 91); Tim Street-Porter (credits appear on page 126); Steve Vierra (credits appear on page 95); Eric Roth (credits appear on page 14).


Printed in China.

# Dedication

Dedication

Dedicated to my sisters, Donna Hamilton and Suzy Blanchet, who have realized their dreams of country living—one on a lake in the Ozark hills, the other in the high mountains of Wyoming.

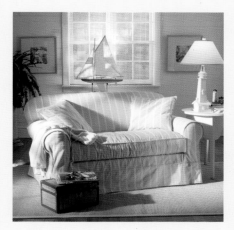

# Acknowledgments

Acknowledgments

I extend my sincere thanks to the entire staff at Rockport Publishers, and in particular to two remarkable women. Acquisitions Editor Rosalie Grattaroti conceived the idea of the *Room By Room* series and invited my participation from the very beginning. As always, her great spirit and refreshing perspective on life make working with her a joy. The book's editor, Martha Wetherill, is a master of her craft—a graceful editor blessed with a patient, even-tempered nature. Madeline Perri's sensitive copyediting also sharpened the text. In a book as visual as this is, excellent graphic design is critical. Argus Visual Communication came through with nothing less.

Thanks, too, to the many interior designers, architects, and photographers whose work is featured on these pages. Their creative energy is at the heart of this book, expressed in a broad range of country rooms.

Finally, my heartfelt gratitude goes to Susan Fockler and Pennington Brown, who so generously shared their idyllic country cabin on North Haven Island in Maine. While there last summer—in between gazing at windjammers on the horizon, listening to the song of the white-throated sparrow, and gathering wild raspberries growing just outside the door—I began writing *Room By Room: Country Interiors*.

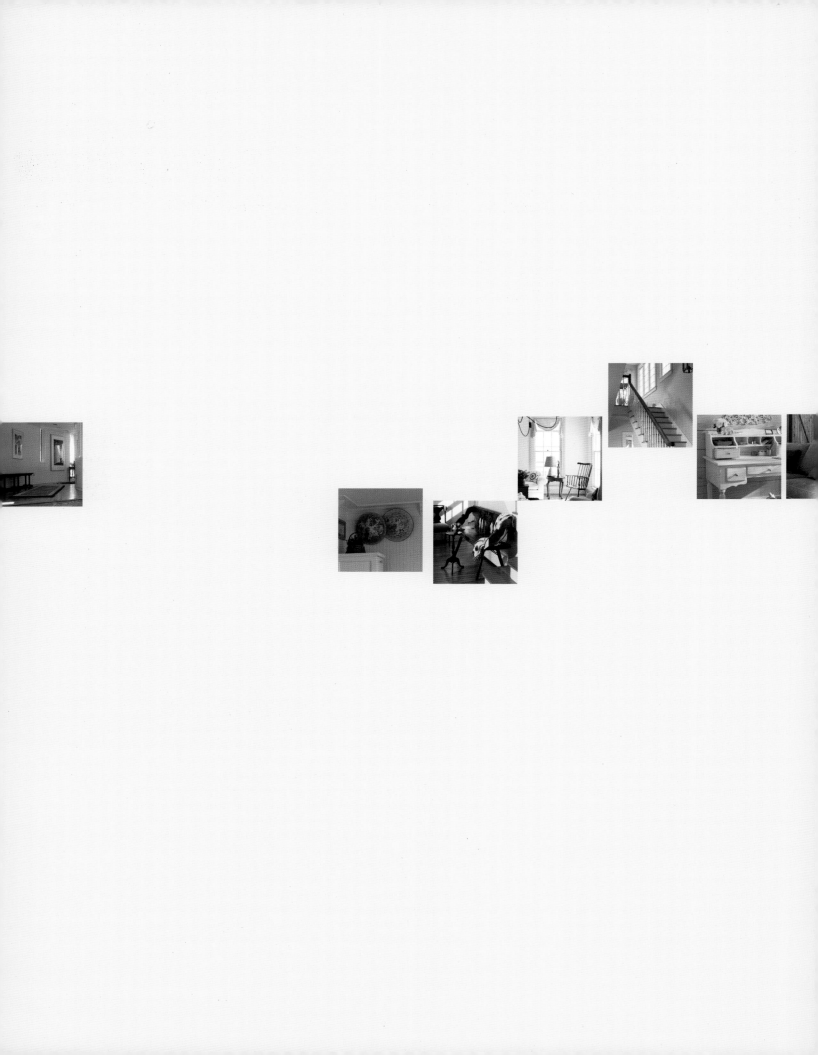

# Contents

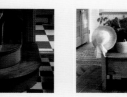
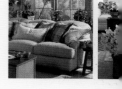

# Foreword

Elizabeth Klee Speert

Since I began my career as an interior designer in 1979, I have seen country style gradually evolve into today's individualized expressions of home that blend antique and contemporary elements in a comfortable, easygoing way. The unpretentiousness of the country approach—its kick-your-shoes-off-and-come-sit-awhile spirit—appeals to a wide spectrum of people. Many of my own clients, ranging from rock stars to business moguls, gravitate toward a country look.

But country style means something different to each person. In fact, country is not so much a distinct style as it is an attitude, in that nearly every period or geographical decorating style lends itself to a country variation characterized by a casual sensibility. For some, the term primarily means the simple lines of Scandinavian whitewashed furniture. For others, it connotes primitive American pieces or rustic Adirondack furniture. For still others, *country* evokes visions of a French château filled with slightly distressed furniture and elegant but worn fabrics. As a designer seeking to create interiors that reflect each client's personality and tastes, I appreciate this endless variety of interpretations.

My own personality has an irreverent side, so I also appreciate country's welcoming attitude toward experimentation and whimsy. In my country retreat, a cabin in southwest New Hampshire with lake and mountain views, I give impulse free rein. Exploring local junk shops and antiques stores, I buy objects that seem right for the setting, collectibles that will carry memories of afternoons spent treasure hunting on back roads. Because country style is so accepting, my collections of unmatched fish plates and funky metal and ceramic owls seem right at home in the cabin. I also collect carved wooden Black Forest bears, and every year the population increases so much that I suspect the bears are procreating. Surely I didn't actually *buy* all of those bears!

This proclivity for assembling off-center, whimsical collections has infiltrated my city residence as well. That, I believe, is the seductive, even insidious side of country. Once interior decorators and homeowners become receptive to its charms, this versatile approach becomes harder and harder to keep out. Formality gradually gives way to relaxed comfort, the drive for perfection is replaced by appreciation for the timeworn, and self-consciousness is overcome by happy abandon.

After poring over the tremendous variety of inviting interiors in *Room By Room: Country Interiors*, however, I trust you will agree with me that the spread of country style is not cause for concern but for abundant celebration.

Elizabeth Klee Speert's distinctive interior design work is frequently featured in *House Beautiful, Country Home, Better Homes and Gardens,* and *Decorating.* In addition to having her residential projects published numerous times in *Traditional Home,* she was the 1993 recipient of the magazine's Design Innovator's Award. With an education in acting as well as interior design, Ms. Speert also has presented segments on interior design for daytime television.

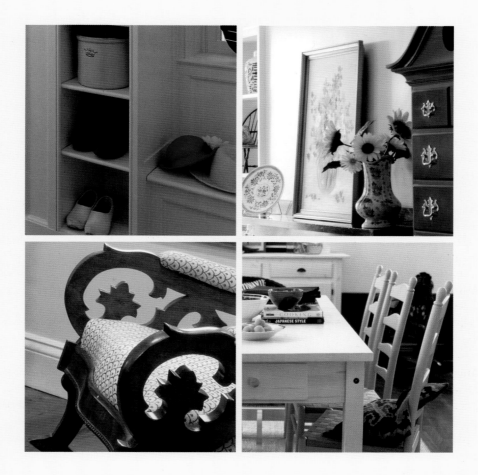

# Introduction

Hearing the words *country style* transports most of us to another time, another place. For some, thoughts of summer days spent at a charming lakeside getaway come to mind. Others think of a rough-hewn log cabin in the mountains, an adobe-style hut in New Mexico, or an old stone farmhouse in southern France. For me, the word *country* evokes memories of the Midwestern farmland my forebears homesteaded. There, I spent halcyon childhood days immersed in the wonders of the garden and barnyard, and sweet nights sleeping under quilts made by my grandmother and great-aunt.

Aside from personal associations, though, the very idea of *country* holds promises of retreat and renewal. As a style, it is every bit as much about mood and attitude as it is about place and time. People drawn to a country style of interior design—whether they are decorating a home in a metropolitan, suburban, or true rural setting—yearn for simplicity and warmth, honesty and lack of affectation. In their personal environments, they tend to be romantics hoping to transcend the hard-edged modernity of our high-speed world.

Indeed, country style's growing popularity in the past few decades has coincided with the rise of the high-tech age. Sometime in the 1970s, those quilts I slept under as a child—along with country style in general—made it big in decorating circles. World-class interior designers began incorporating folk art, regional textiles, and worn painted furniture into clients' homes. In the United States, the nostalgia of the 1976 bicentennial celebration fueled the trend. Soon, quilts and primitive tables were populating the pages of upscale magazines that previously eschewed anything vaguely uncosmopolitan.

During the past thirty years or so, all kinds of regional and national variations on country style have gained definition and popularity well beyond their geographical homes. Within each genre, numerous subsets have emerged, from rustic cabin, to modest cottage or farmhouse, to the refined country manor style. American country has long been associated with the colonial underpinnings of the classic New England look. Other regional styles now get their due, too, such as Western ranch style, featuring lodge-pole furniture and cowboy-theme accessories, and Southwest style, with its affinity for large-scale patterns, light woods, Spanish influences, and adobe architecture. Native American crafts and textiles are at home in both of these regional variations. Several styles with strong historical ties also fall under the heading of American country, including the pure forms and exquisite craftsmanship of the furniture made by the Shakers.

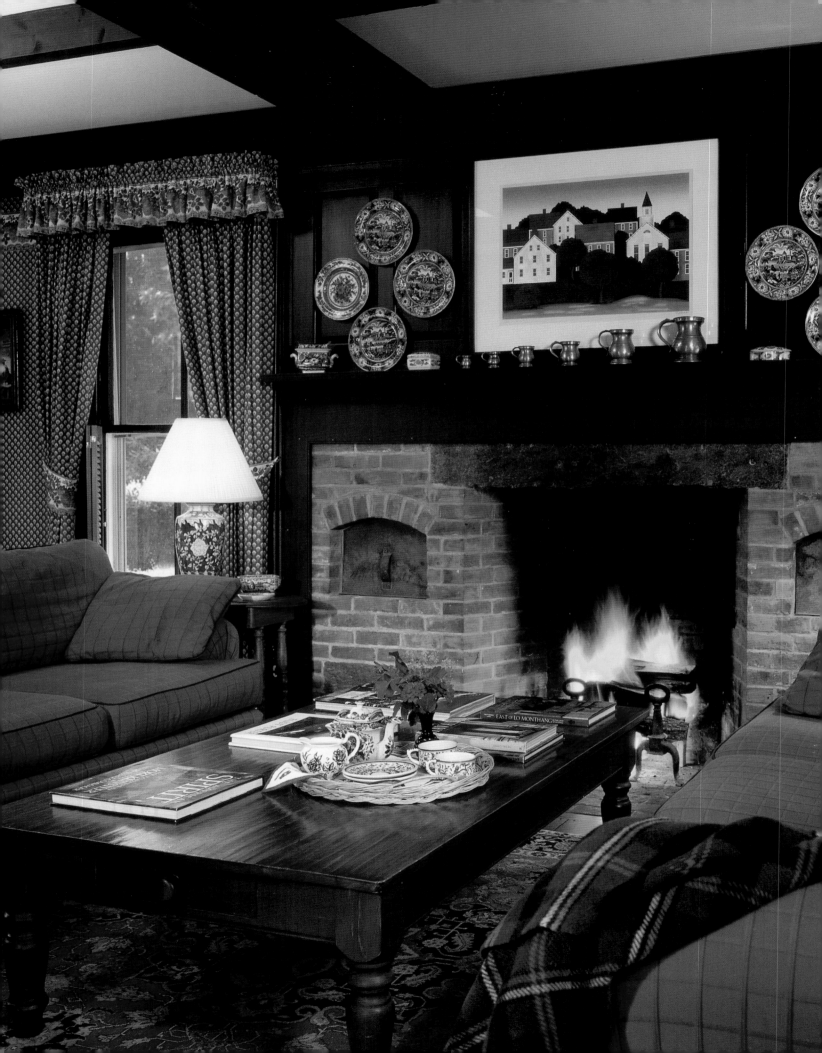

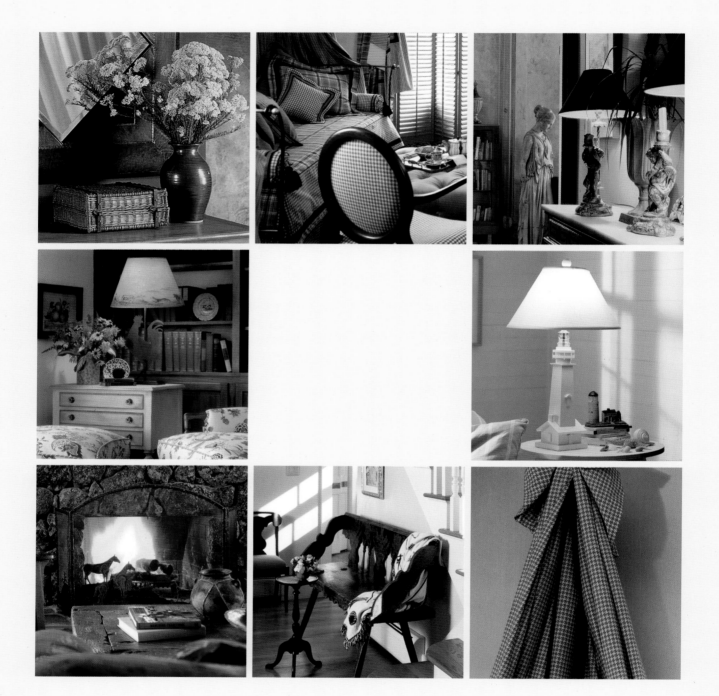

Numerous European country styles have gained renown as well. English country, with its floral chintzes, cluttered coziness, and slightly worn quality, has made Anglophiles out of millions. French country includes vernacular versions of period furniture popularized in monarchs' courts, as well as delightful fabrics such as toiles depicting pastoral scenes. Many people equate French country with the regional style of sunny Provence, characterized by pure colors, small-print cottons, and terra-cotta stone floors. To the north, Scandinavian country style offers a crisp palette, pale painted furniture, and beautifully textured woven rugs.

The list of variations goes on, with attention recently turning to colonial styles from as far afield as the West Indies, Indonesia, and Hawaii. But the most important of the latest trends has to do not with geography but with overall approach to country style.

First, the relaxed attitude of eclecticism, the carefree mixing that has revolutionized all kinds of design, is infusing country style with easygoing aplomb. Rather than setting out to decorate a room within the confines of one strict genre, people who love the country look now feel free to blend together a variety of regional elements. Gone are any qualms about pairing a Provençal print, for instance, with a country Swedish daybed. Contemporary furniture, lighting, and textiles also are welcome in country rooms. The only caveat is that a room's designer still must take into account fundamental aesthetic considerations such as scale, texture, pattern, color, shape, and balance.

The second major change in the style is a pendulum swing away from the excessive, over-the-top clutter that permeated so many homes in the past few decades. In the new country style the bywords are *lean* and *clean*, which allows architecture to come to the forefront. Rather than filling every surface with collections, the new country style involves conscious restraint. Through careful editing, the special qualities of furniture and accessories are individually celebrated: the patina of an antique table, the quirkiness of a piece of folk art, the rich texture of each homespun textile. The result of pared-down design, say advocates of this approach, is rooms that make people feel more organized and peaceful. Lightening up, after all, can be good for the soul.

As *Room By Room: Country Interiors* is a patchwork of interpretations of country style, think of the myriad images on the following pages as pieces of an Amish quilt. Practitioners of a simple way of life, the women of the strict Amish religious sect sometimes leave a blank space in the midst of their intricately patterned quilts. The opening, they say, provides a place through which the spirit can enter.

This book is designed to inspire your unique spirit to enter in as you create your own country-style home.

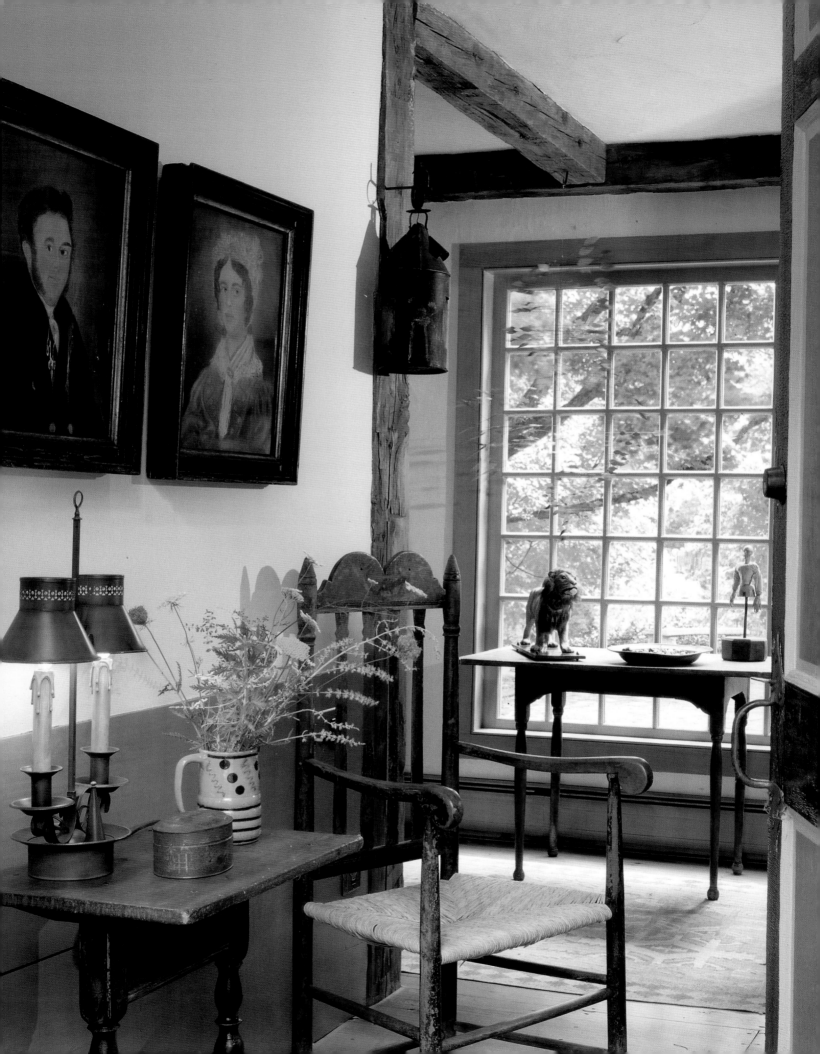

# *Country* Entrances

*The journey is as important as the destination; so goes the popular saying. In terms of country houses, the journey into the heart of the home takes place in the residential equivalent of highways and byways: transition spaces such as entrances, stairwells, and halls.*

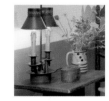 While these areas are intended primarily for movement, never underestimate their potential impact on those who pass through. Stairwells and halls, with their expansive walls, can be transformed into effective galleries for artwork and family portraits. Transition areas, punctuated by doorways leading to a home's essential spaces, also frame views into interior rooms. As a result, well-designed halls that enhance views through door frames create an easy visual flow from one space to another.

The entry hall provides the first glimpse of a home after one steps through the front door. Choose colors and an aesthetic that complement the rest of the house, both inside and out. If your style is the simplified approach of new country, then keep the entry hall spare, too. If adjacent rooms have the look of an English gardener's cottage, a bouquet of fresh peonies and a colorful hooked rug will provide hints of what is to come. And don't pass up an opportunity to showcase special passions in the entry hall: framed prints of songbirds, for instance, or dried wild grasses collected on autumnal strolls. The more personality an entrance reveals, the better.

Keep in mind, too, that entries are places for shedding and putting on coats and boots, hats and mittens. In casual country interiors, these things become part of the decor, with denim jackets and straw hats hanging from plain pine pegs or an antique oak hall tree. Various sizes and colors of boots lined up on a shelf have down-home appeal. If space allows, don't forget to provide a bench as a temporary resting spot for people, groceries, school backpacks, or the day's mail. Country life, after all, is active and engaged with the outside world.

This hospitable entrance, newly built with antique materials, seamlessly joins a 1720 Connecticut farmhouse with a spacious addition. The mobile, an unexpected contemporary element, brings color and movement to the space.
Photo: Eric Roth

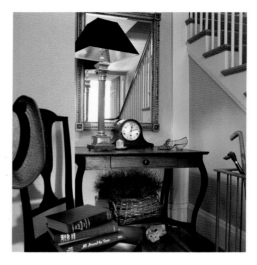

Sophisticated elements such as a mantle clock, elegant lamp, and gold-framed mirror are mixed with country touches—a straw hat, basket of dried flowers, and china cat—to create an inviting entrance hall. Design: Laura Crosby Photo: Steve Vierra

A back entryway leading to a porch and garden is sponged verdant green like outdoor foliage. Red accents and a rooster lamp and pillow complement the room. Design: Debra Jones Photo: Tim Street-Porter

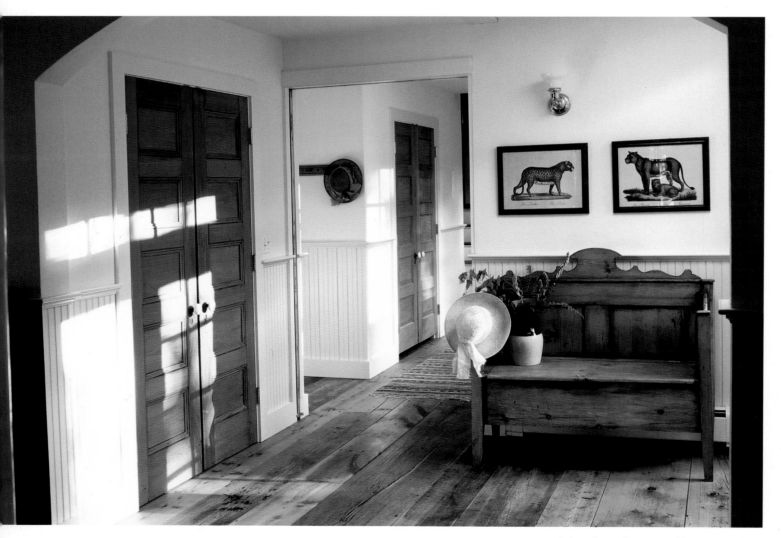

A duet of neutrals—ivory and brown—provides a serene backdrop for welcoming friends and family to this Nantucket home. White walls and bead-board wainscoting show off the rich patina of the rough-hewn floor, paneled closet doors, and antique settee. Design: Mark Hutker & Associates; Photo: Eric Roth

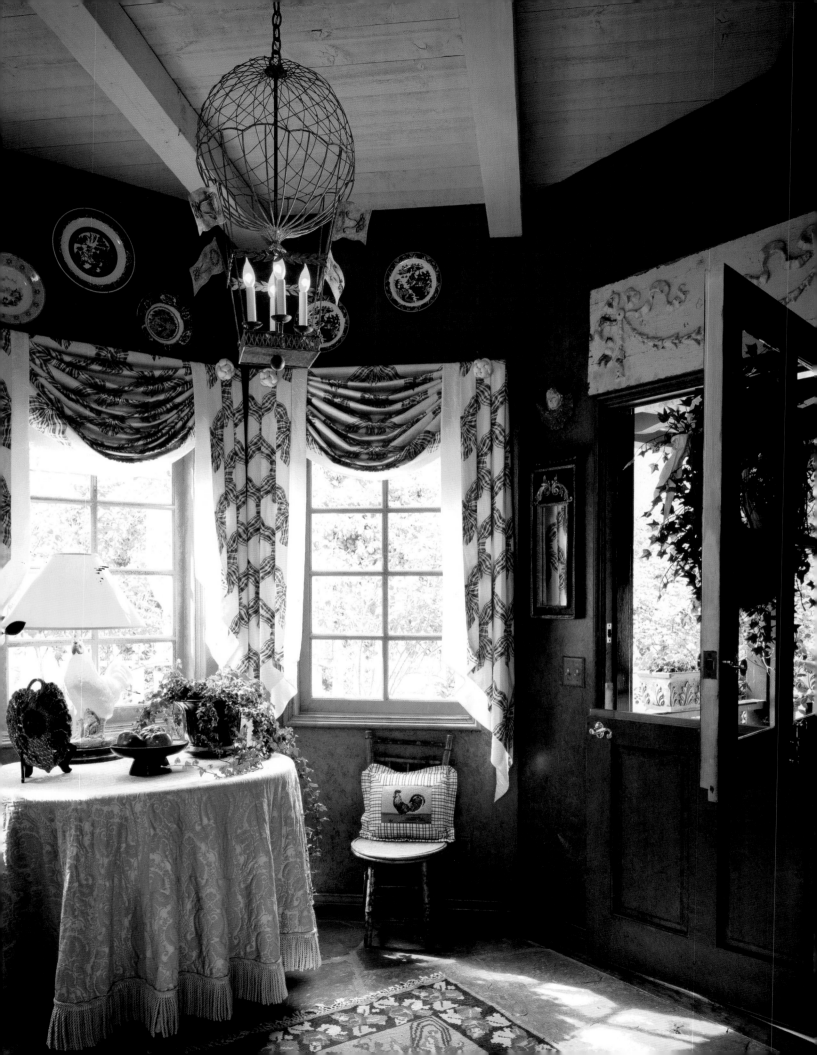

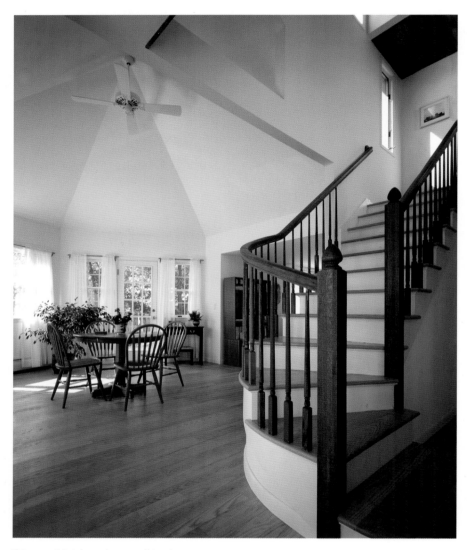

This graceful stairway has a traditional balustrade, but the overall architecture and refined decoration place it in the context of updated country style. Design: Thomson Architects; Photo: Wade Zimmerman

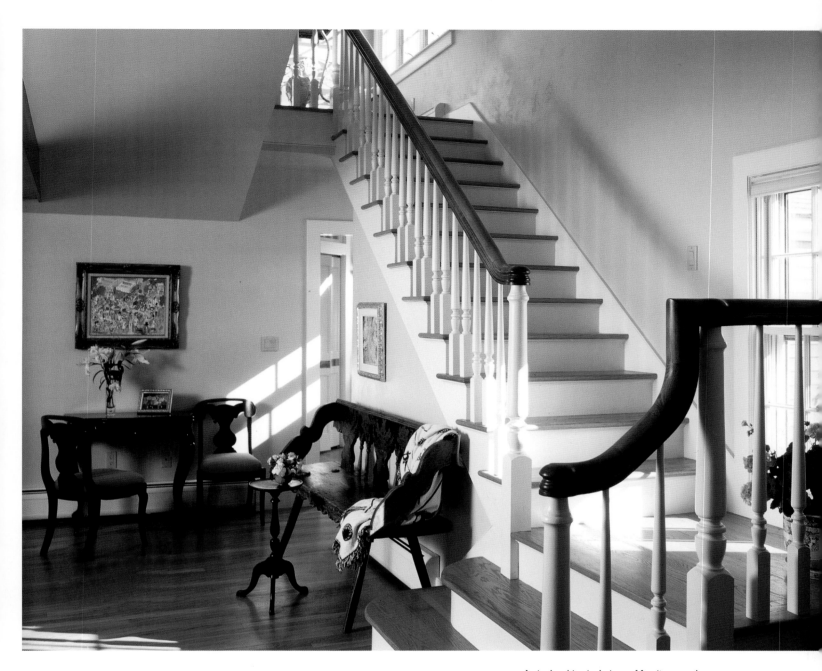

A single whimsical piece of furniture, such as a one-of-a-kind folk-art bench, completely changes the tone of even the most traditional entry halls. Windows without curtains—a feature of the current style—allow sunlight and shadows to move across the space. Design: Kalman Construction Photo: Eric Roth

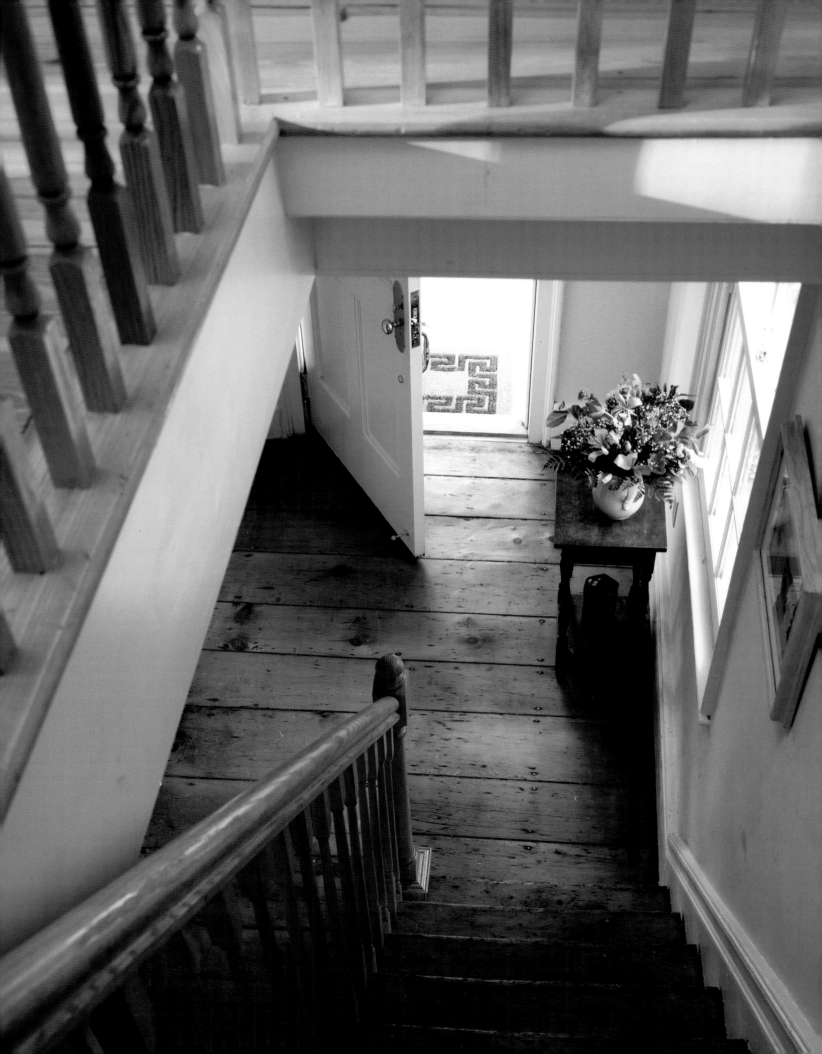

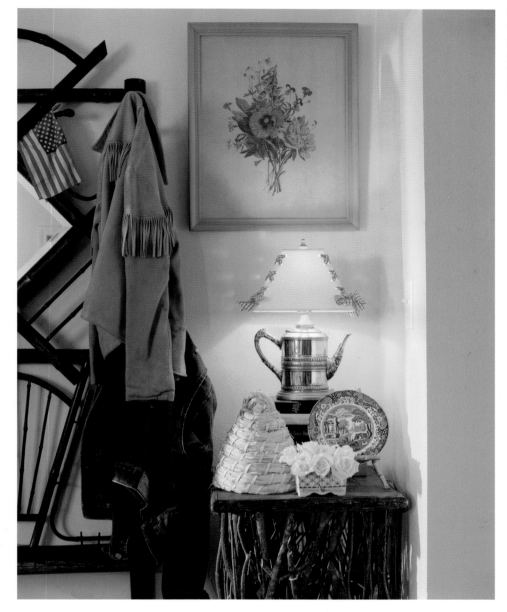

Rustic furniture brings the spirit of the frontier to this entry. On the twig table, a small straw bee skep shares space with touches of refinement: yellow roses, blue-and-white porcelain, and a lamp with a silver coffee pot base and ribbon-laced shade. Photo: Jean Allsopp

The essential charm of this entry and stairway comes from exposed antique pine floors prized particularly for their unevenly worn boards and distress marks. Design: Gustavson/Dundes
Photo: Peter Paige

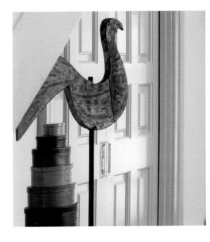

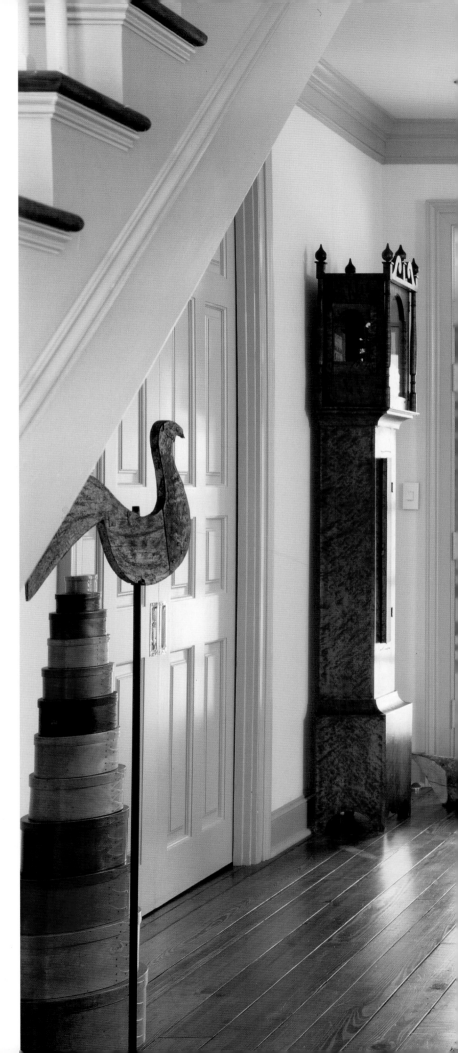

Natural illumination is often in short supply once the entryway door is closed. Extending fanlights (above the door) and sidelights to nearly the height and width of the entry hall floods this country manor entrance hall with daylight, showing off stained pine floors and a pewter collection displayed in a country hutch.

Photo: Tim Street-Porter

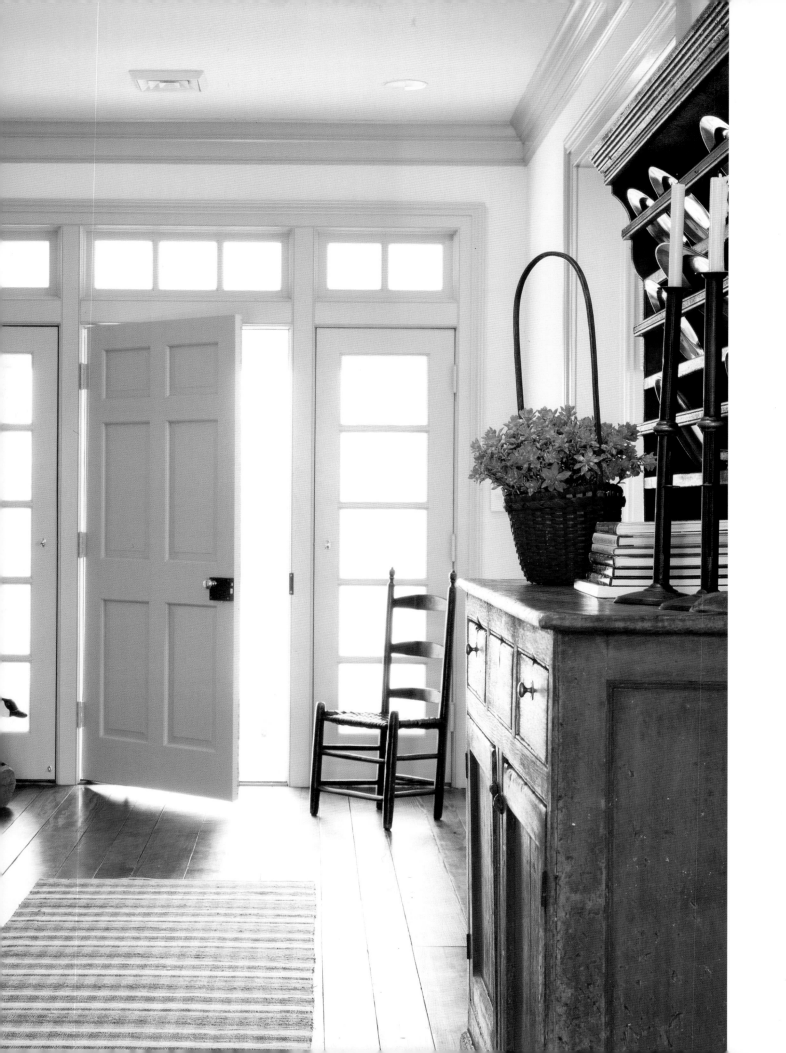

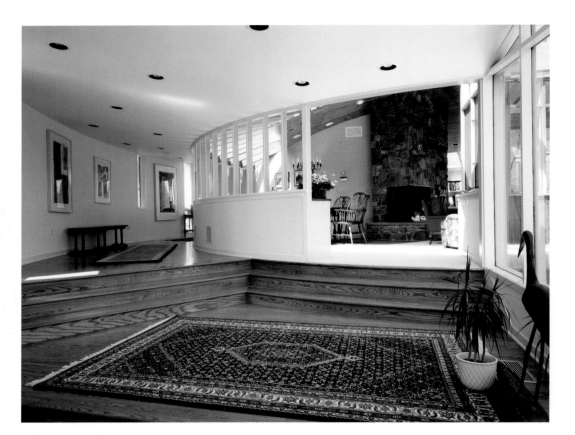

In this new country entry, contemporary architecture draws the eye to a stone fireplace and curved hallway. Established focal points—whether architectural or decorative— draw people in like a gesture of hospitality.
Design: Lester Korzilius Architect
Photo: Wade Zimmerman

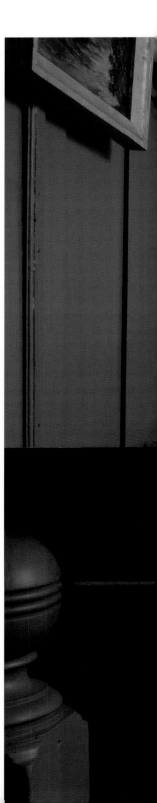

A joyous mingling of collectibles and decoratively painted surfaces draws visitors into the eccentric vestibule. One of the owner's loves is immediately evident: reading and collecting books.
Photo: Eric Roth

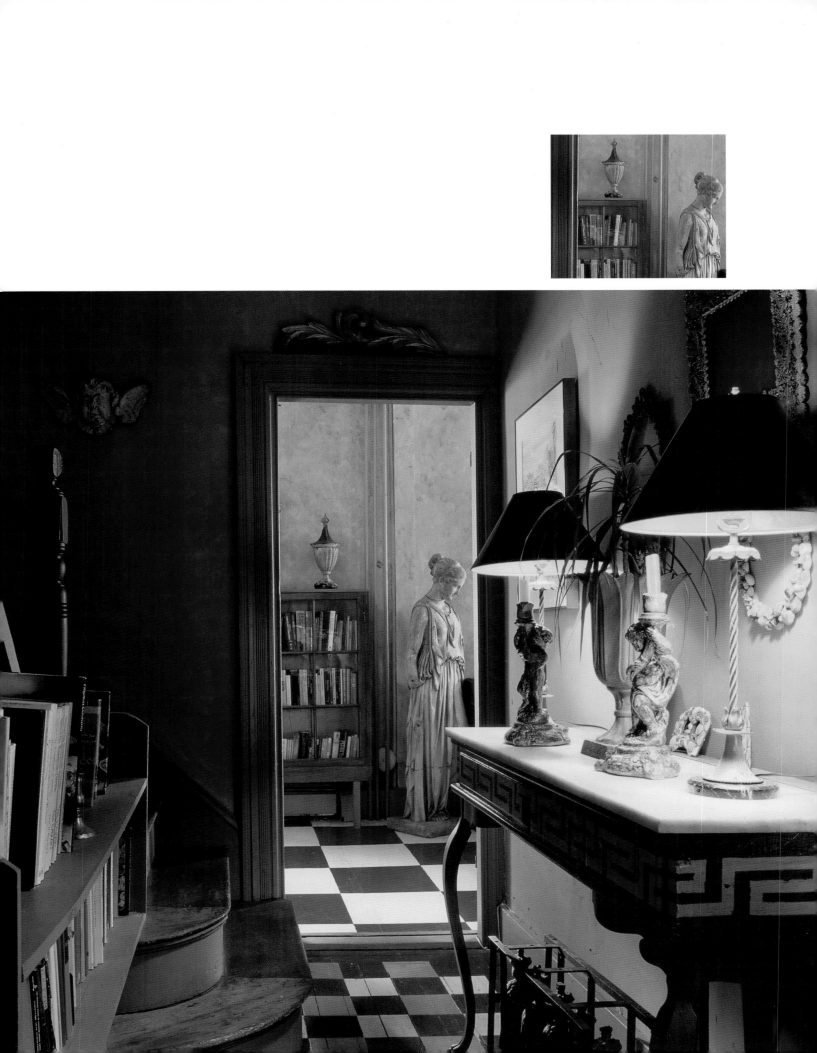

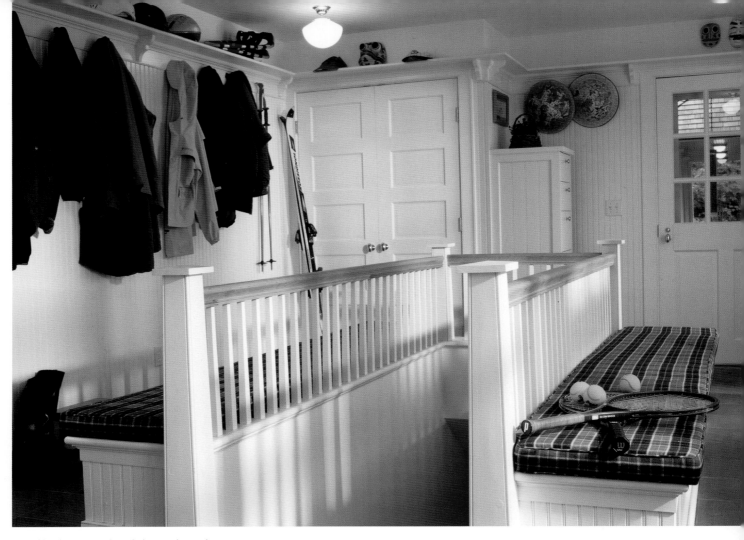

Active families accumulate clothing and gear that can be accommodated by a well-planned back entry hall complete with hooks, shelves, drawers, closets, and benches. Design: Austin Patterson Disston Architects; Photo: Jeff McNamara

Today's country entrances and stairways, rather than being cluttered, rely on one or two focal points for effect. A massive wooden fish and a second-story window with diamond-shaped panes are simple yet striking. Design: Kalman Construction; Photo: Eric Roth

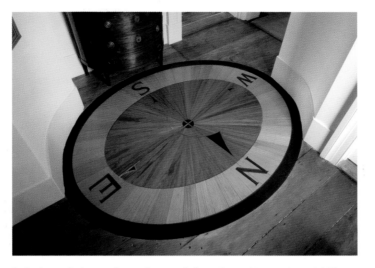

In the foyer of a historic house that once belonged to a ship captain, an inlaid compass rose points the way to a new addition. Design: Austin Patterson Disston Architects; Photo: Fred George

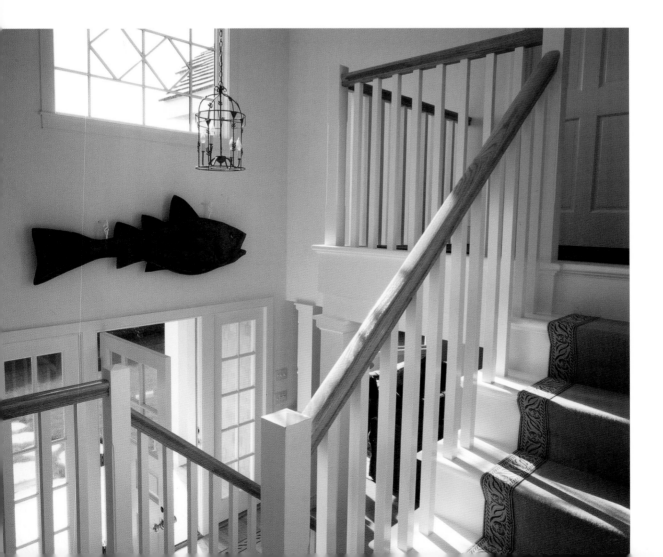

This back entryway immediately opens into a delightful riot of collected objects. A painted armoire provides storage amid a room teeming with vivid colors and curious objects.
Design: Tony Duquette; Photo: Tim Street-Porter

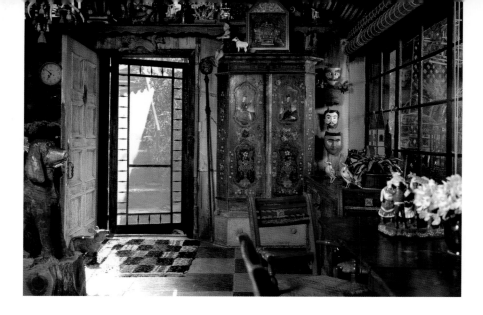

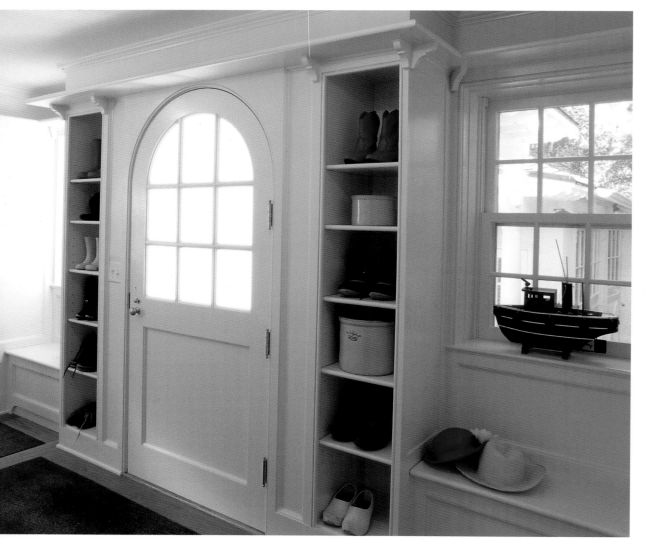

Shelves flanking a side door are great for organizing boots and shoes, whose myriad colors and shapes give the impression of a deliberate collection. Adjacent lift-top benches provide additional storage. Design: Austin Patterson Disston Architects; Photo: Robert Benson

The teal of the distinctive front door is echo throughout this Southwestern cottage. The and unique style of the door emphasize the transition between inside and outside, ever in the absence of a separate entry hall.
Photo: Tim Street-Porter

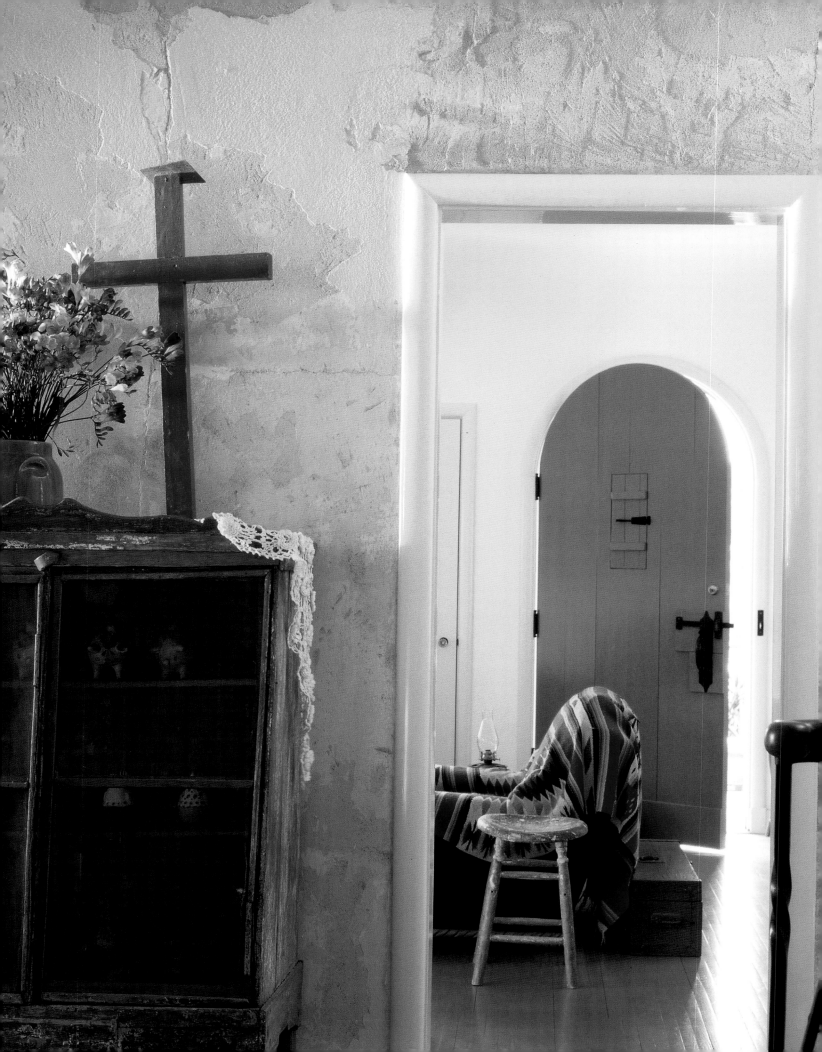

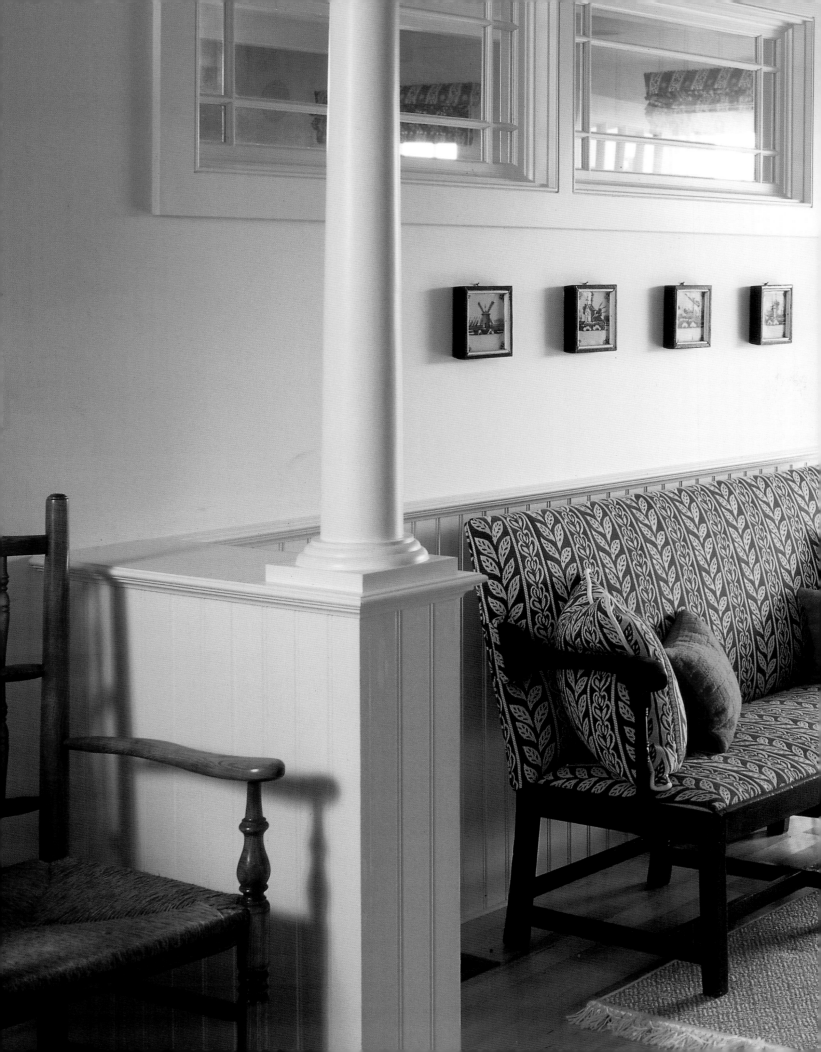

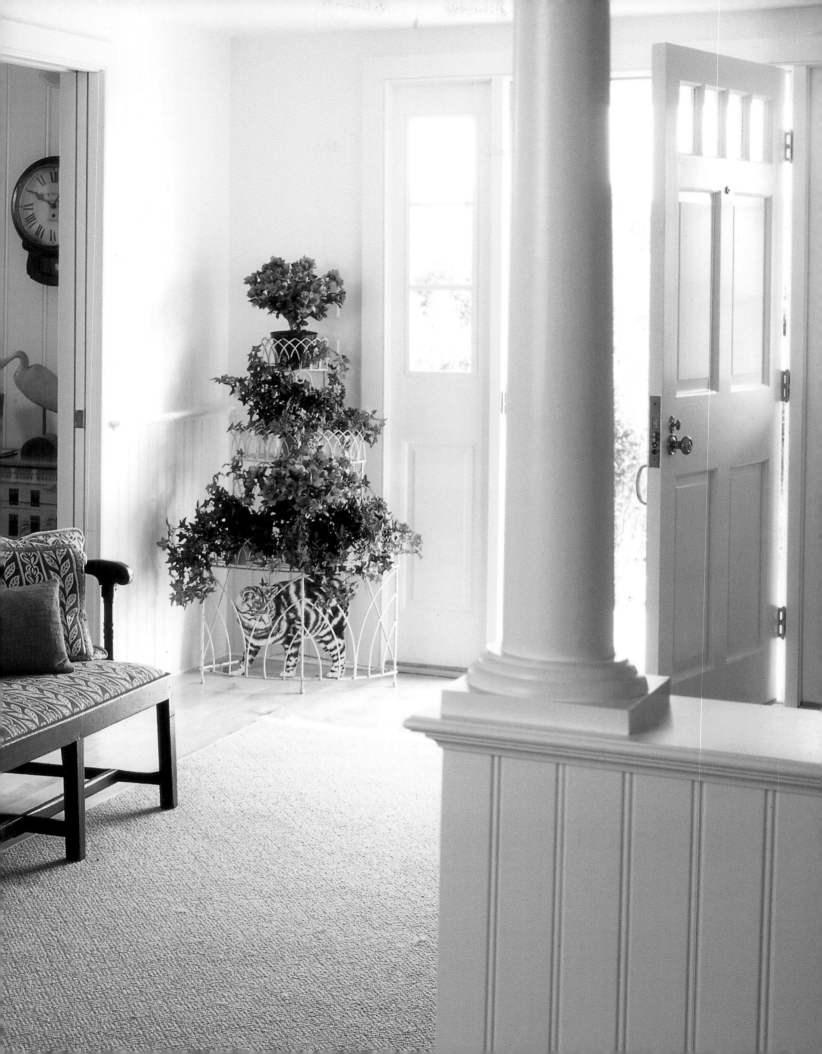

Previous pages: The new country ambience of this broad foyer is due to its light and airy feeling and its openness to the rest of the house. The style's playfulness comes out in the striped cat sculpture hiding below the plant stand. The blue of the settee is echoed in the framed Delft tiles above. Design: Kalman Construction Photo: Eric Roth

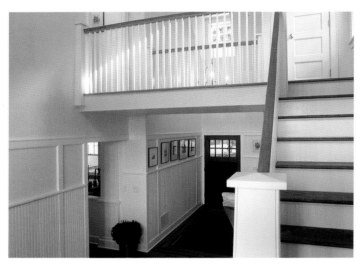

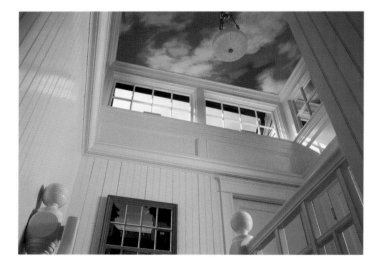

Top: Walls with bead-board wainscoting, always a popular country look, are dressed up with additional molding above the wainscot. The resulting squares and rectangles form a gallery-like setting for displaying framed art and photographs. Design: Austin Patterson Disston Architects; Photo: Jeff McNamara

Bottom: This stairwell offers three creative ideas for adding interest to an often neglected part of houses: a realistic painting of a window with a delightful seaside scene, a cloud-filled sky painted on the ceiling, and, to the right of the clerestory windows, a window frame with mirror glazing. Design: Elizabeth Klee Speert Photo: Eric Roth

Back entryways often are hardworking, as in ranch room that even offers a sink for cleani up after a day in the great outdoors. The gre cabinetwork's rustic iron hardware mingles fortably with spurs, lariats, and a trio of woo hens roosting behind chicken wire. Design: Barbara Barry; Photo: Tim Street-Po

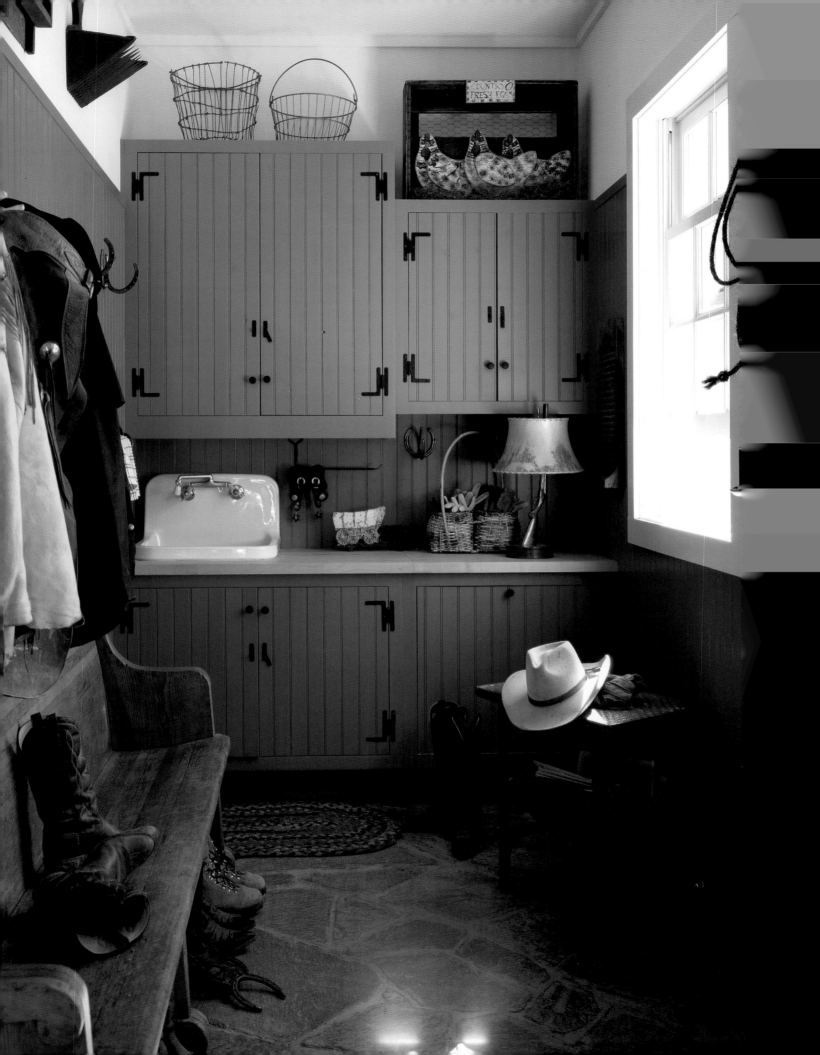

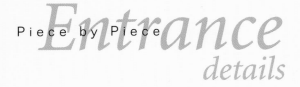

*Convey a distinctive personal touch through entryway details such as a basket of favorite wildflowers or an unusual mirror or artwork. Table lamps and sconces—aesthetically pleasing, yet extremely practical—welcome guests to your home with a warm glow. When putting all of the pieces together, plan storage for the accoutrements of outdoor life—hats, boots, and jackets.*

*Lighting the Way*

Creating a sense of warmth is essential to country style, so include table lamps and wall sconces in entry halls to provide inviting golden light (below).

*Floral Arrangements*

Set out a lush bouquet of fresh-picked flowers arranged in a simple antique pitcher or fill a cachepot with yellow roses to signal hospitality to everyone who enters the front door (below).

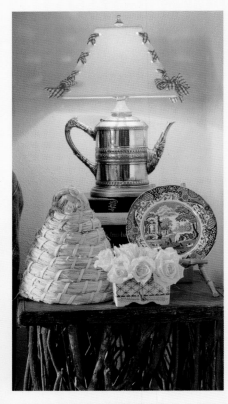

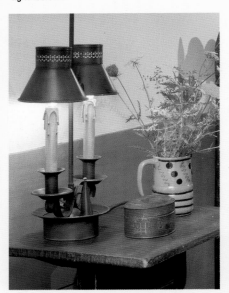

*Hang-Ups*

Hat racks and coat trees evoke the casual attitude appropriate for country interiors (below).

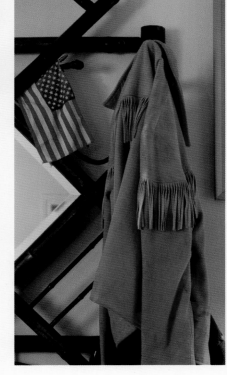

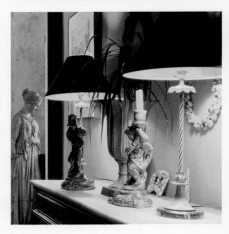

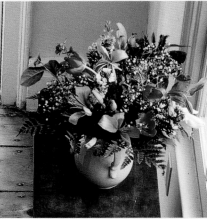

An entrance hall spacious enough to accommodate a bench or settee can provide a welcoming seat and convenient storage for hats, scarves, and gloves (below).

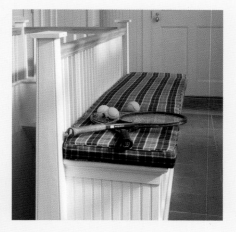

*Setting the Tone*

Choose entryway objects that set the tone for the rooms beyond. A playful checked rug, animal doorstop, and carved dog tell visitors to expect a whimsical mix. A mirror, such as this Argentinian ranch-style mirror framed in hand-tooled leather hung in an entrance hall, is a functional addition that immediately conveys a home's style (below). Photo of mirror by Kenton Robertson, courtesy of Milling Road

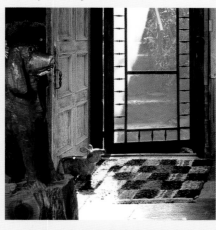

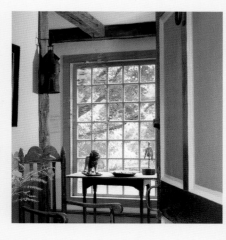

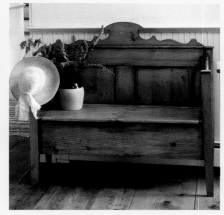

*Finishing Touch*

Coordinating the exterior door with the interior design reinforces the visual impact of the entrance area (above).

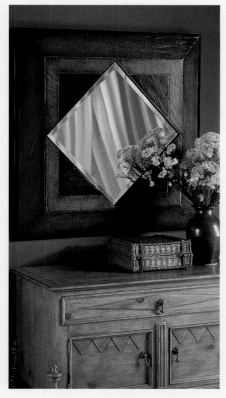

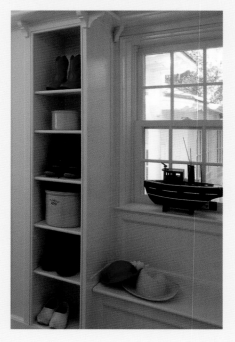

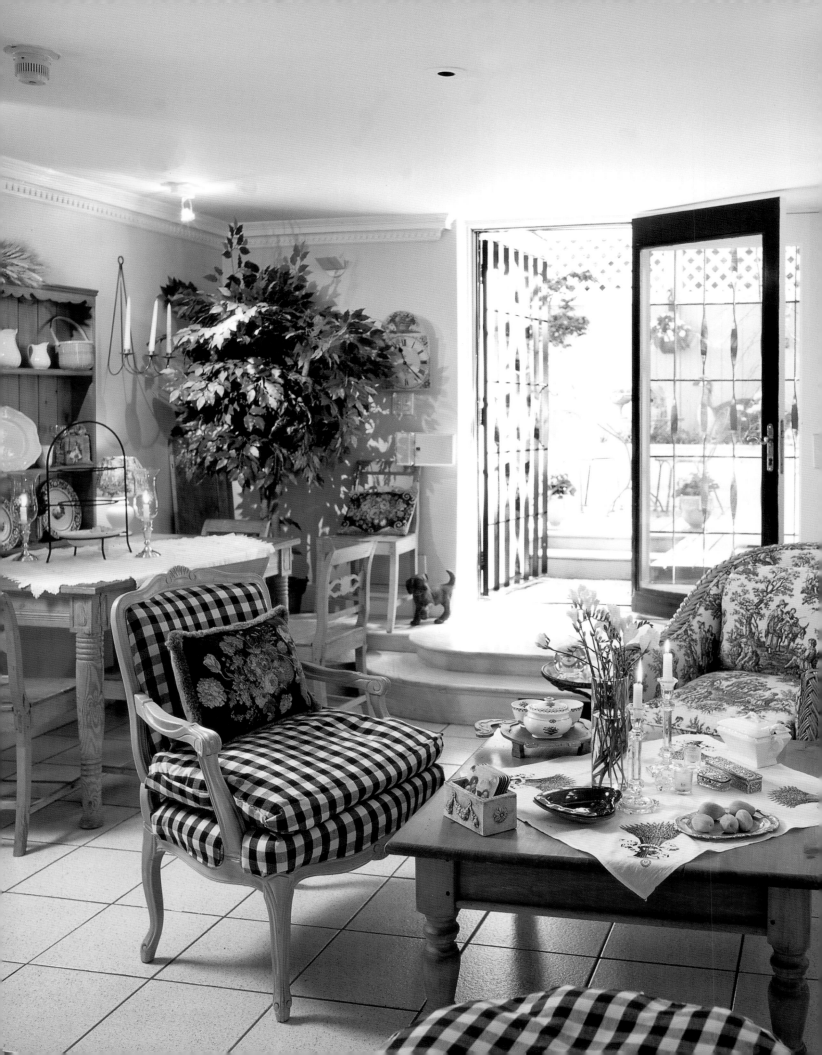

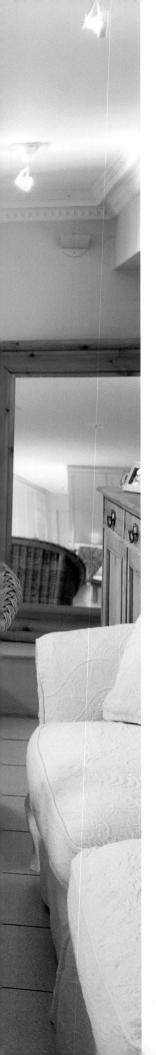

# *Country* Living Rooms

*Country living rooms once were stiff, reserved for formal entertaining. Recent designs make day-to-day use the priority. Here you can share meandering conversations with loved ones or curl up on a deep-cushioned sofa with a cup of tea while listening to music.*

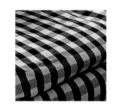

Most country living rooms boast a hearth, that essential element in everyone's fantasy of a home centered on the simple life. Thus the room draws family and friends with a promise of warmth and warm feelings. Here the demands of necessary tasks are replaced by a gentle mellowness; the compulsion to always be *doing* gives way to simply *being.*

Carefully considered furniture and lighting set the scene for a wide range of pastimes. Style is a worthy concern, but planning for practicality is even more important than whether you choose the polished attitude of a refined country manor or the rustic look of a cabin in the woods. If the living room isn't hospitable, comfortable, and easygoing, the point of country is missed.

First, make the room physically welcoming with amply stuffed furniture that encourages people to sink in and relax. Seating should be flexible—ideally,

a grouping to accommodate six people, plus extra chairs if needed. Consider where beverages will be placed, perhaps on a wicker tea caddy or an old blanket chest used as a coffee table. Attractive and functional lighting is another vital design aspect. Window coverings are important for providing decorative interest through texture and pattern and for moderating daylight.

Plan a focal point for the living room. In addition to focusing on fireplaces and woodstoves, you might also group seating to center on a curved bay window that opens to a pastoral view, or arrange furniture to emphasize the coziness of a vintage hooked rug.

Storage is an integral feature of living rooms that work well. Plan a place to tuck away toys and games—perhaps a steamer trunk or corner cabinet. Integrate a television and other electronics with care, preferably hiding them away behind cabinet doors. Gather books into the room, stacking them on tables and shelves to display well-worn spines.

**A black-and-white scheme, often used in modern interiors but rarely in country ones, gives this room a twist. The wicker chair's upholstery is toile, a distinctive fabric originating centuries ago in France, which depicts romantic pastoral scenes.** Design: Constance Driscoll Design Consultants; Photo: Eric Roth

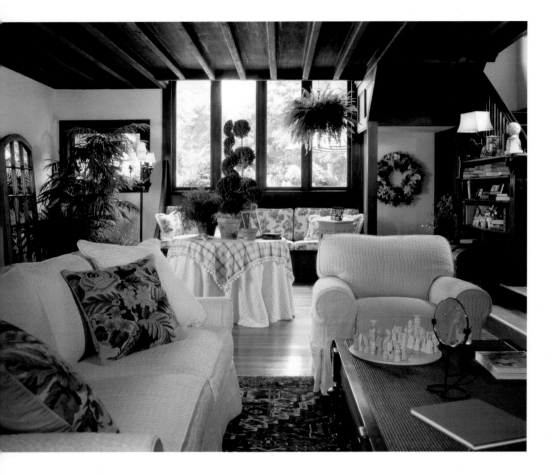

A massive stone fireplace and open-beam ceiling blend with the ivory-upholstered chairs and sofa for an easygoing yet refined decorating style. A window seat (above) offers a secondary activity area, perfect for reading or a tête-à-tête. The light-colored walls and fabrics brighten what could be a dark room. Design: Judy Collins and Bob Collins, Peach Tree Designs; Photos: Steve Vierra

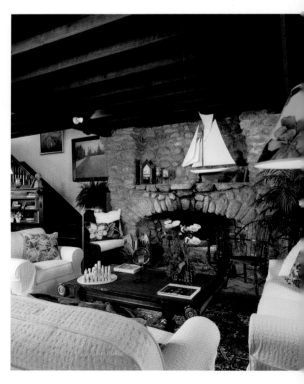

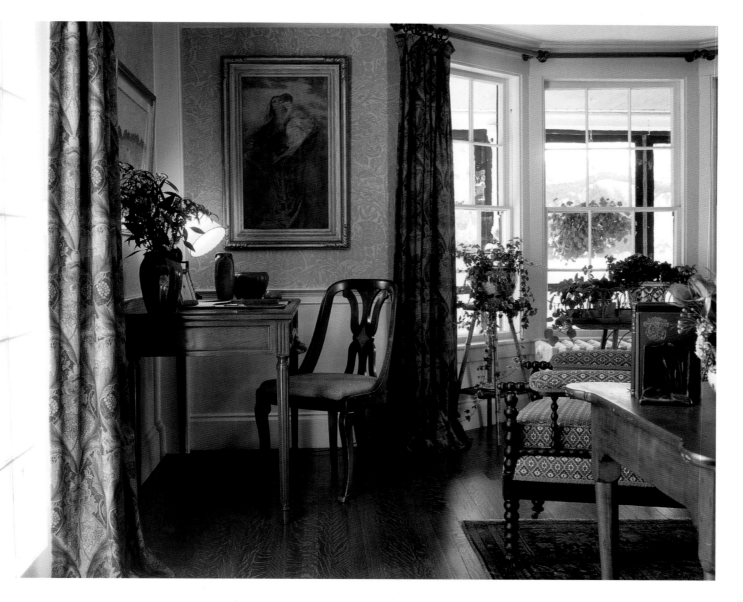

Liberal mixing of floral patterns, upholstered furniture, and eclectic antiques gives this living room the English country look embraced in recent years by homeowners all over the world. A writing desk in a quiet corner (above) is the perfect spot for keeping up with correspondence, an activity no doubt punctuated by an occasional daydream. Design: Marisa Morra, Artistic and Historic Interiors
Photos: Steve Vierra

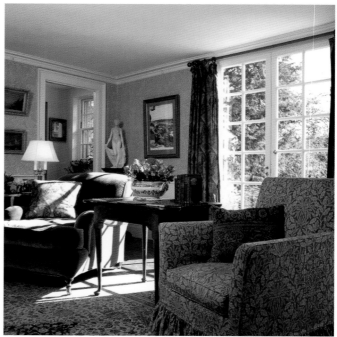

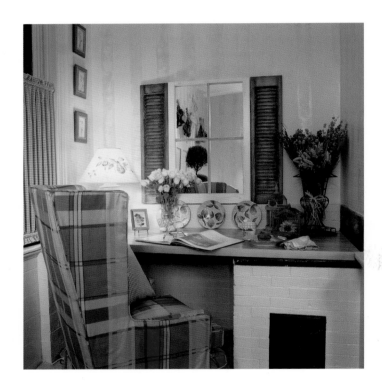

Yellow, green, and rose tints add to this pretty sitting room's cheerful atmosphere. A botanical theme—abundant bouquets, fruit patterns on lampshades, and upholstery fabric—pervades the space. Design: Pamela Karlyn Mazow

Photos: Peter Jaquith

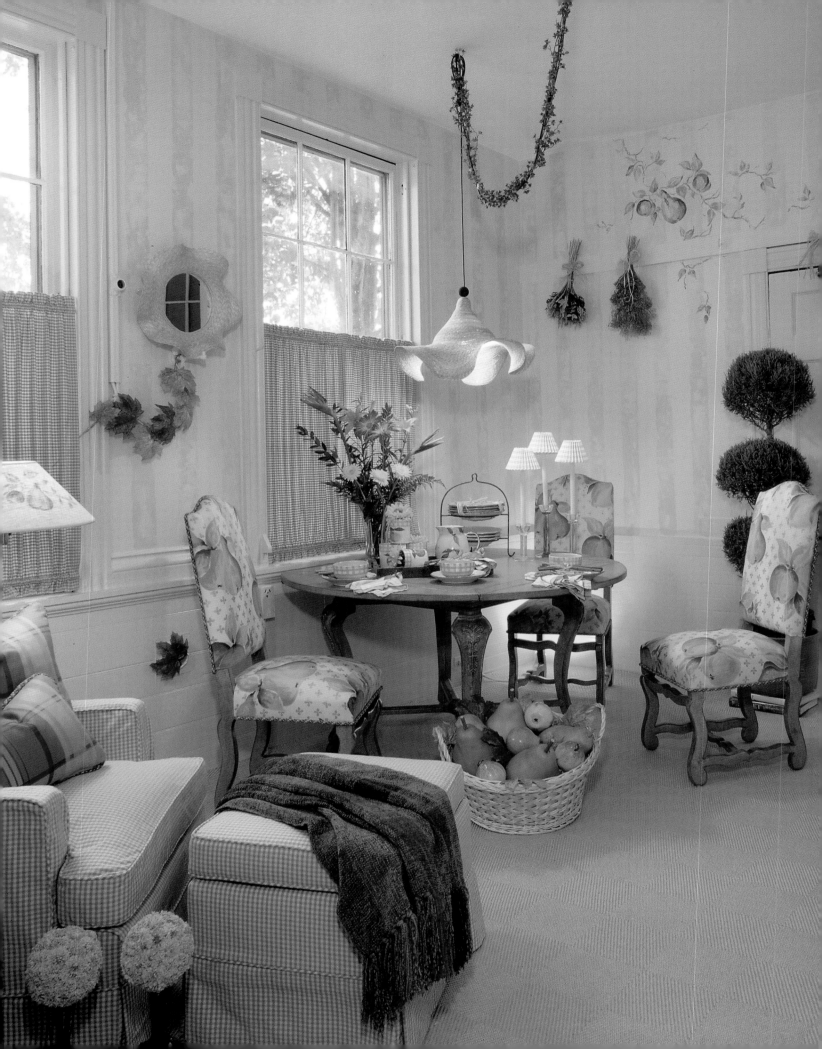

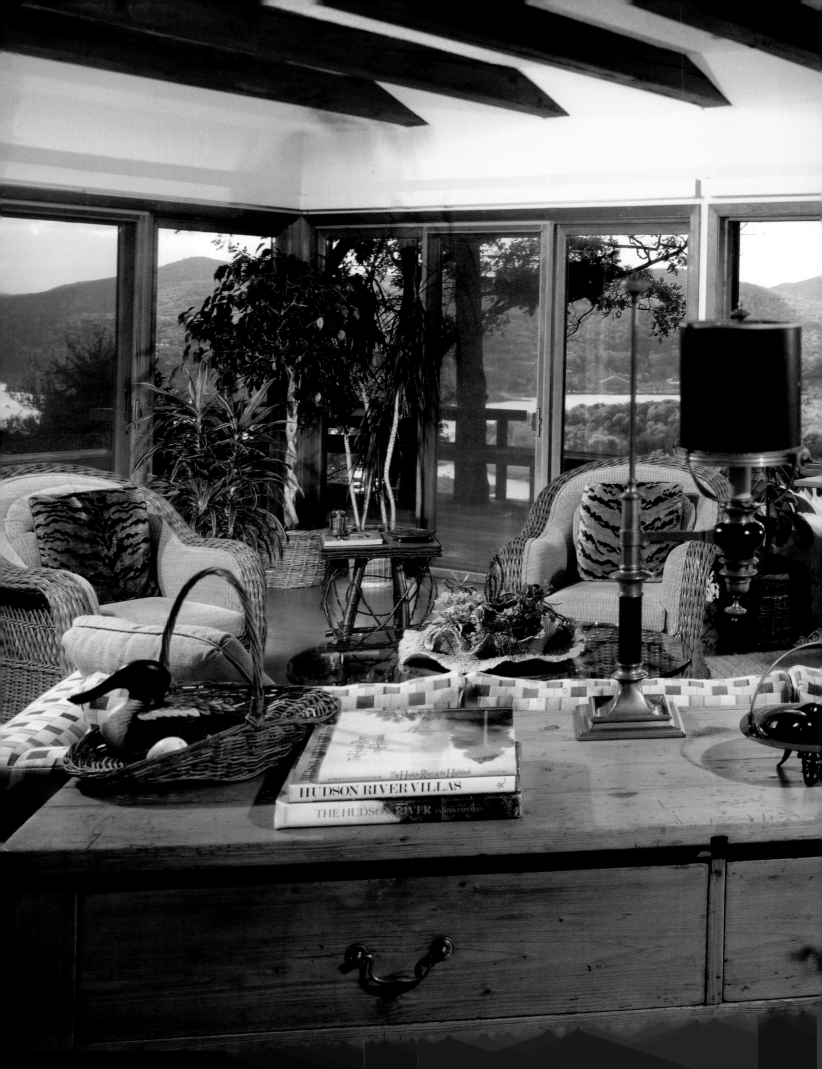

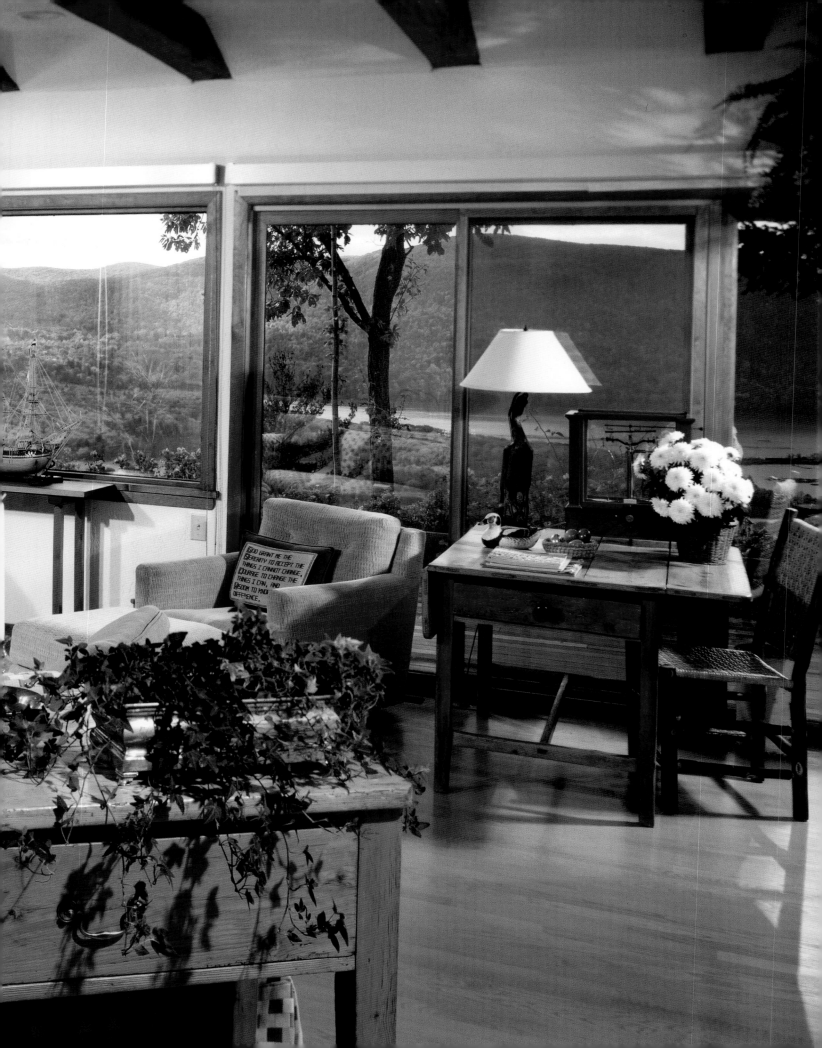

Previous pages: A judicious use of pattern and
a palette of neutrals provide a soothing, unde-
manding ambience that yields center stage to
the beauty of outdoor scenery.
Design: Martin Kuckly; Photo: Bill Rothschild

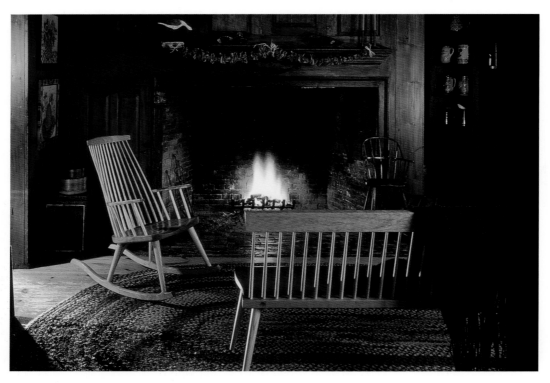

In antique houses, chairs and settees with graceful, simple lines honor the historic architecture.
A braided rug is a favorite floor covering in
American colonial style. Photo: Paul Rocheleau,
courtesy of Thos. Moser Cabinetmakers

The vibrant colors and geometric patterns of th
kilim carpet and sofa upholstery add warmth a
energy to this cozy living room, providing a
snug, secure feeling on wintry days.
Design: Anthony Antine; Photo: Bill Rothschild

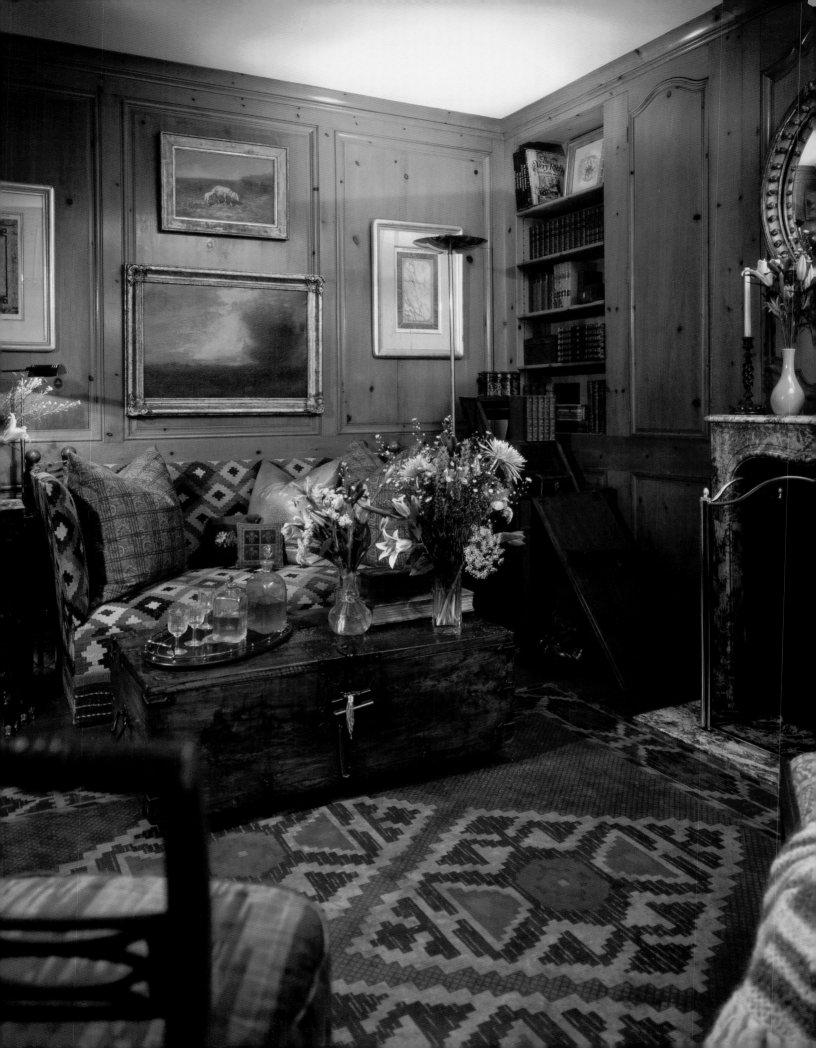

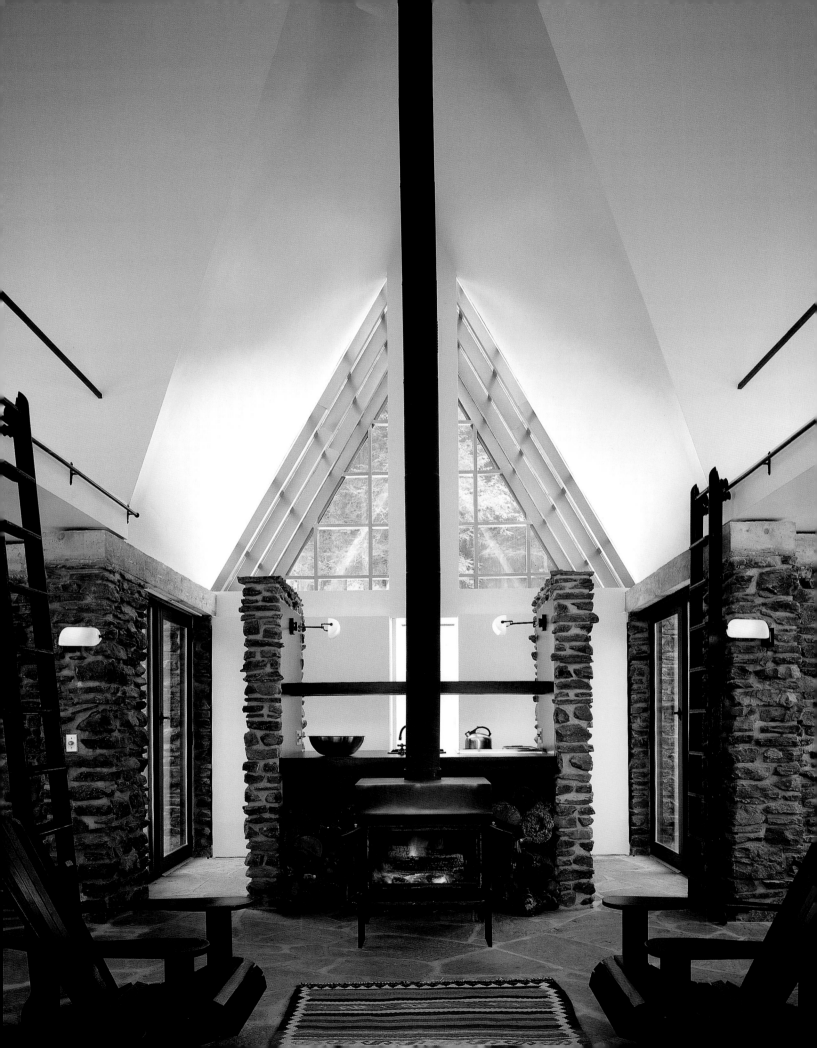

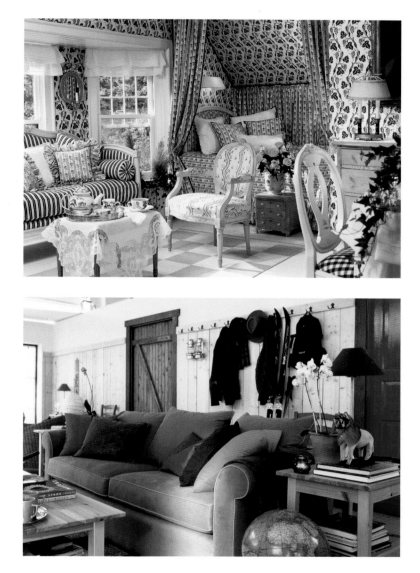

Top: The distinctive flair of this traditional Swedish country room derives from painted furniture and crisp, highly patterned fabrics in blue and white.
Photo courtesy of Country Swedish

Bottom: Unfinished pine, with its humble lack of polish, is a natural choice for an unaffected mountain ski retreat. Brightly colored pillows and painted doorways are perky additions.
Photo courtesy of IKEA

outside is brought in with natural stonework,
nses of glass, and a ceiling that reaches
rd the sky. Adirondack chairs add to the
se of being outdoors on a stone patio.
ign: Marlys Hann; Photo: Paul Warchol

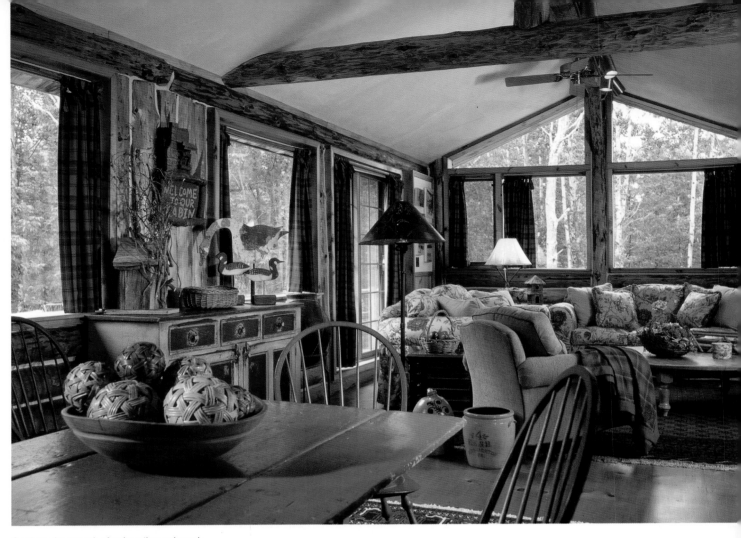

Combine the warmth of red textiles and rough-hewn wood with an open, airy feeling from large windows and lofty architecture. Note how various patterns and designs are brought together in the room—plaid fabrics, floral prints, and intricately woven oriental carpets.
Design: Lillian Bogossian and Vivian Weil, Decorative Interiors; Photo: Steve Vierra

This living room achieves a perfect balance between traditional elements, such as antiqu tables and chairs paired with red-and-white c ed pillows and throws, and new country feat including graphic use of pattern, lack of clutt and a contemporary white sofa and easy cha Photo: Tim Street-Porter

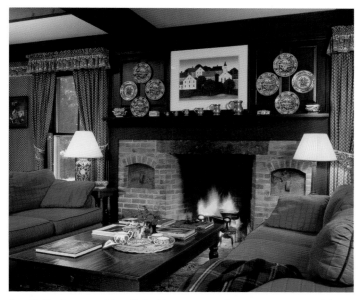

A rustic fireplace complete with beehive ovens, pewter measures on a mantel, and a scene of a colonial village remind one of early New England. Curtains and wallpaper inspired by provincial French designs introduce a slightly different but thoroughly compatible country style. Design: Lillian Bogossian and Vivian Weil, Decorative Interiors; Photo: Steve Vierra

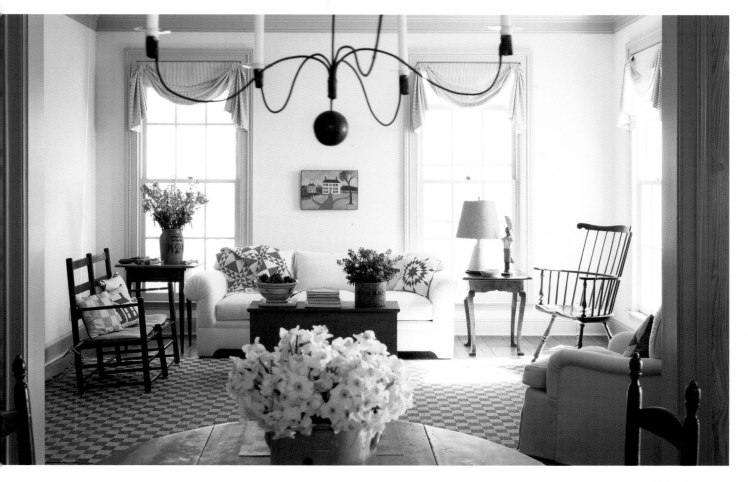

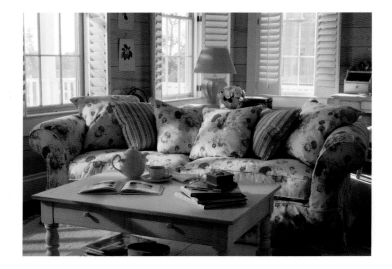

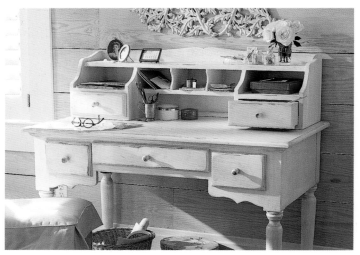

The loose-cushioned sofa invites lounging and the antique-finished writing desk inspires letter writing. In rooms too small for two end tables, put a table lamp behind the sofa to illuminate evenings spent with a favorite novel.

Photos courtesy of Crate and Barrel

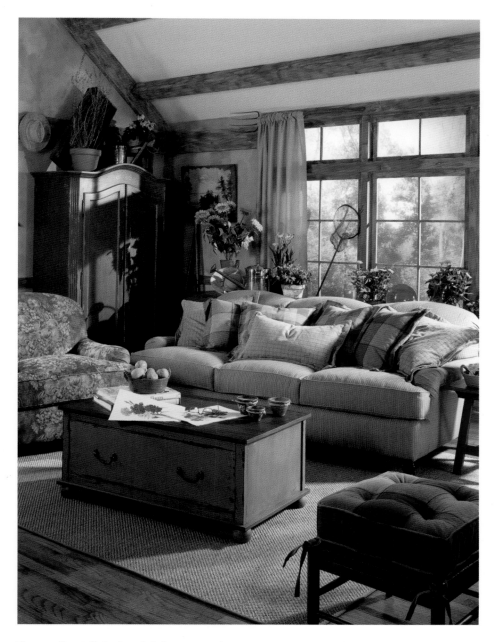

The appealing stuffed sofa and chair are extremely comfortable, which is always a high priority in country style. This room, finished with an armoire and blanket chest, also addresses the need for storage in activity-centered living rooms.

Photo courtesy of Domain Home Fashions

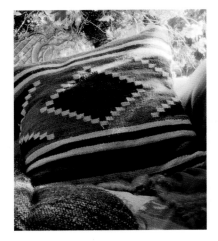

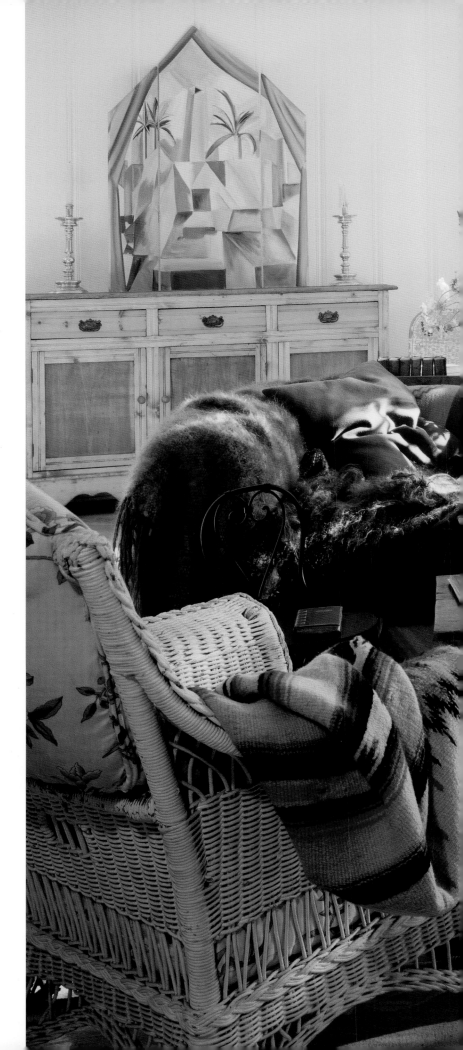

With the casual aplomb of southern California, old wicker chairs and stump-style footstools are gathered around a sofa dressed down with mohair throws and pillows inspired by Native American design motifs. The style is eclectic but essentially country in its affection for worn furniture and mixed patterns. Design: Van Martin Rowe; Photo: Tim Street-Porter

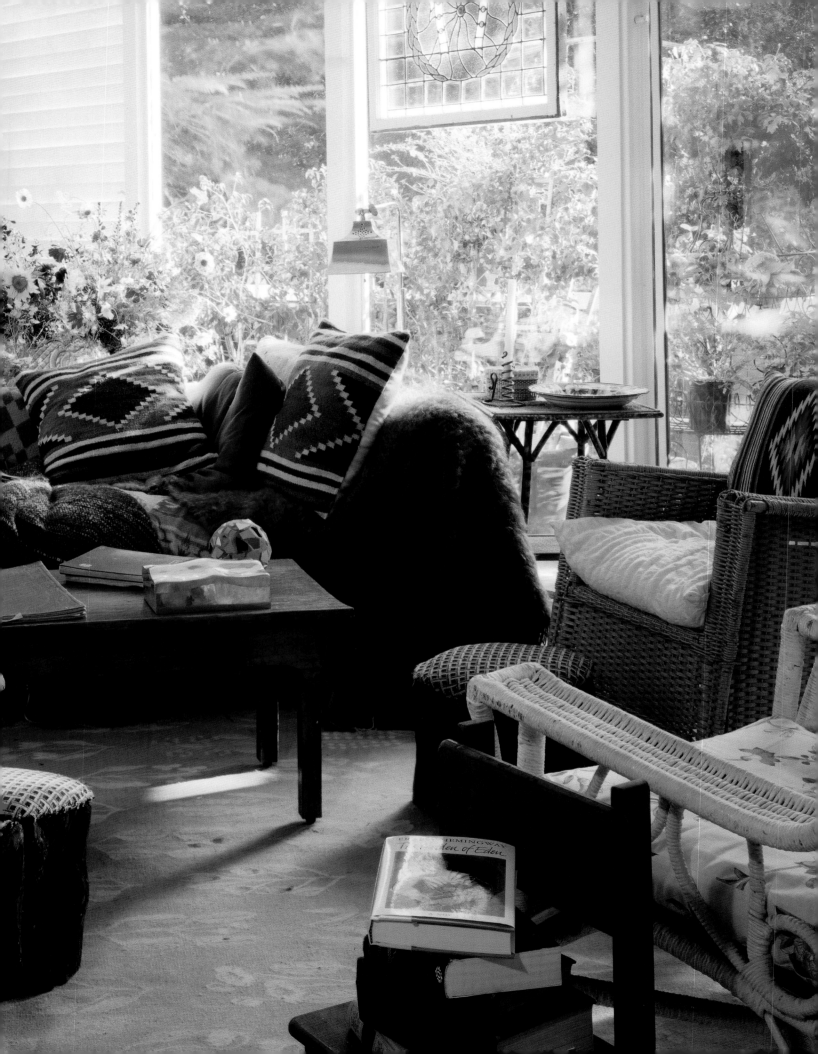

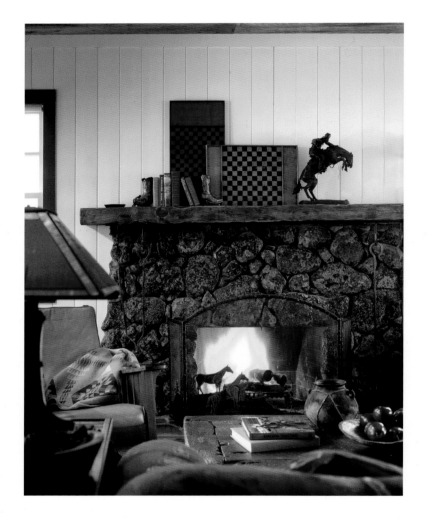

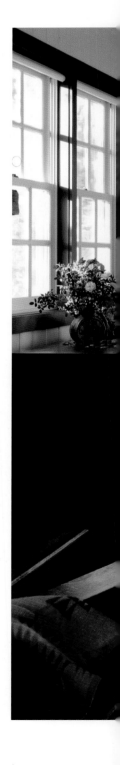

Texture is vital to this Western room's success, from smooth leather chairs to the rugged wooden coffee table and stone fireplace. Intense shades of red and exuberant patterns add visual punch.
Design: Barbara Barry: Photos: Tim Street-Porter

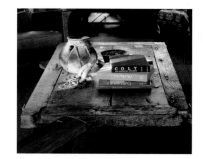

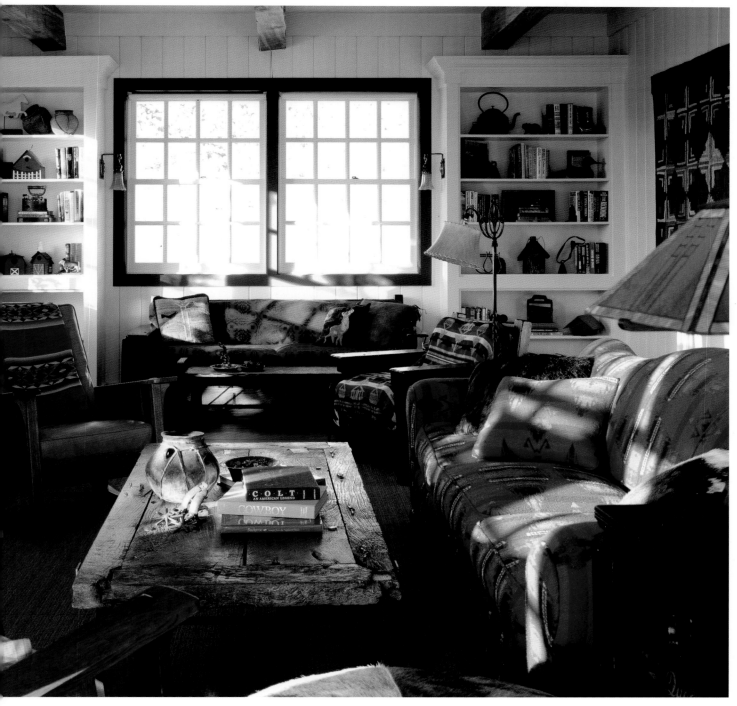

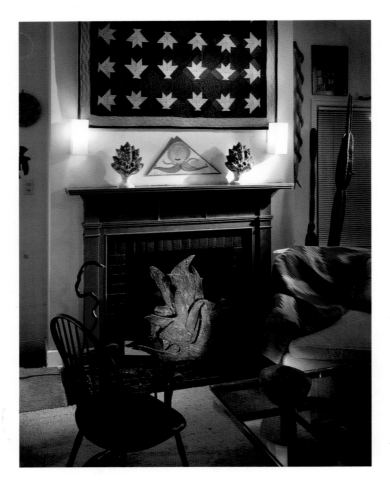

Today's country interiors often include whimsical, quirky elements. Beneath a striking quilt tapestry, a sinuous snake winds alongside a metal sculpture depicting a blazing fire. Photo: Balthazar Korab

The owner of this exuberant living room has a passion for searching out quirky castoffs in obscure junk stores and backwoods barns. The more chipped and cracked a timeworn chair or chest, the more it is prized as a unique treasure. Photo: Eric Roth

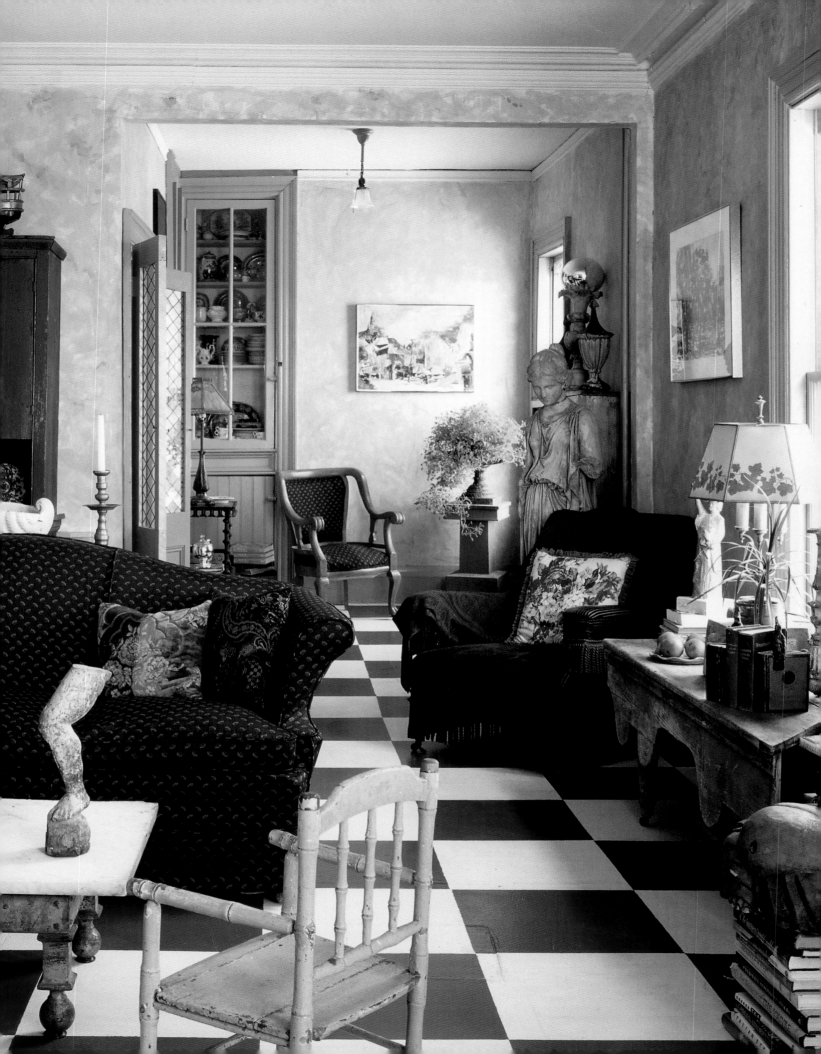

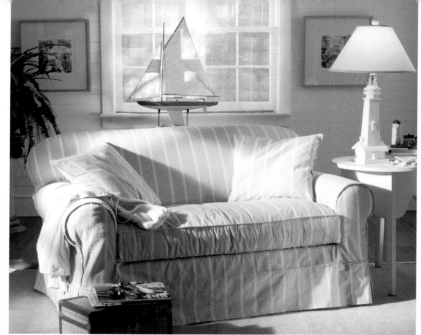

Right: A few accessories with a common theme, such as the nautical imagery here, can give a room distinctive personality. Photo courtesy of Crate and Barrel

New country style gets down to the basics. In this contemporary living room, a simple sofa, large wicker coffee table, and great view are all that's needed. Design: Davis + Maltz Architects Photo: Mikio Sekita

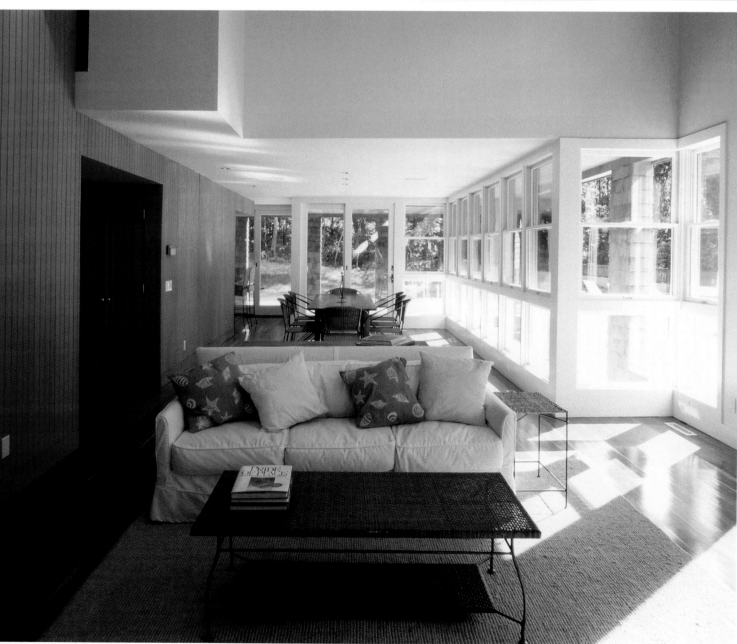

Checked textiles—a classic in homespun interiors—are surprisingly versatile. When a French country manor house's elegant toile draperies and upholstery are juxtaposed with checked accent fabrics, the room becomes more relaxed and free-spirited. Photo courtesy of Pierre Deux

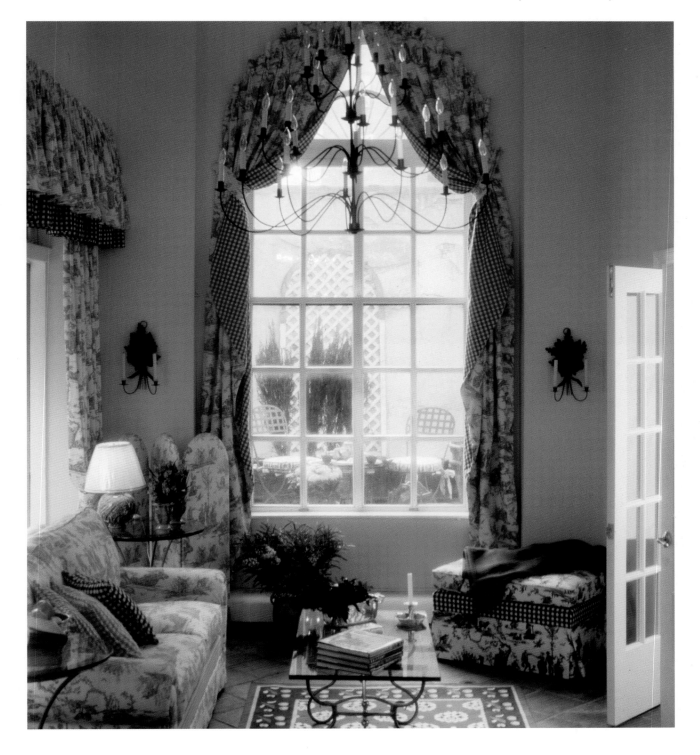

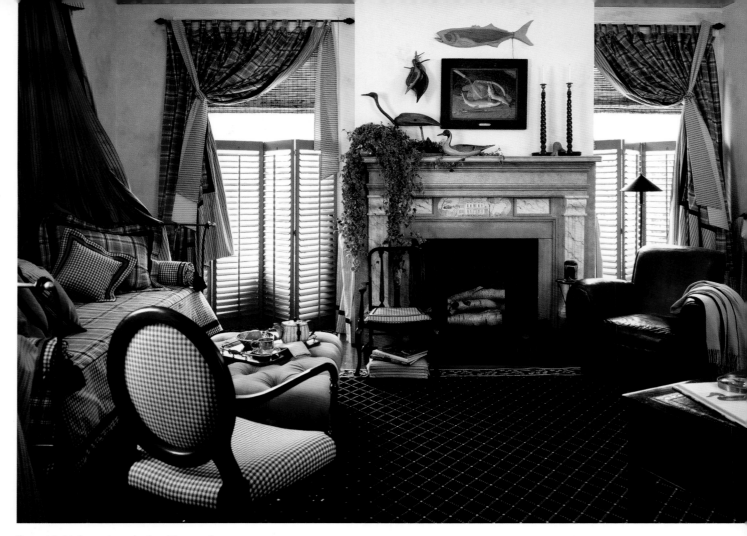

Geometric fabrics such as checks, stripes, and
plaids provide a refreshing tailored alternative to
more traditional floral motifs. Design: Robert
Clark + Raymond LeCuyer; Photo: Bill Rothschild

Clear tones of yellow, blue, pink, and green w
a Mediterranean breeze through this inviting
ner. A touch of whimsy—as in the rooster
lamp—enlivens country interiors.
Photo courtesy of Brunschwig & Fils

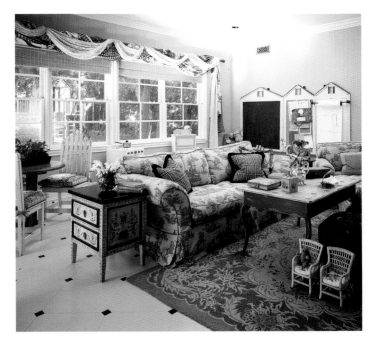

The emphasis is on living in this multifunctional room, where children are more than welcome. Toys are incorporated on the perimeter, where tile flooring is impervious to the effects of chalk dust and "cooking" at the play stove. A braided swag with multiple fabrics is—much like the room itself—pure fun.
Photo: Tim Street-Porter

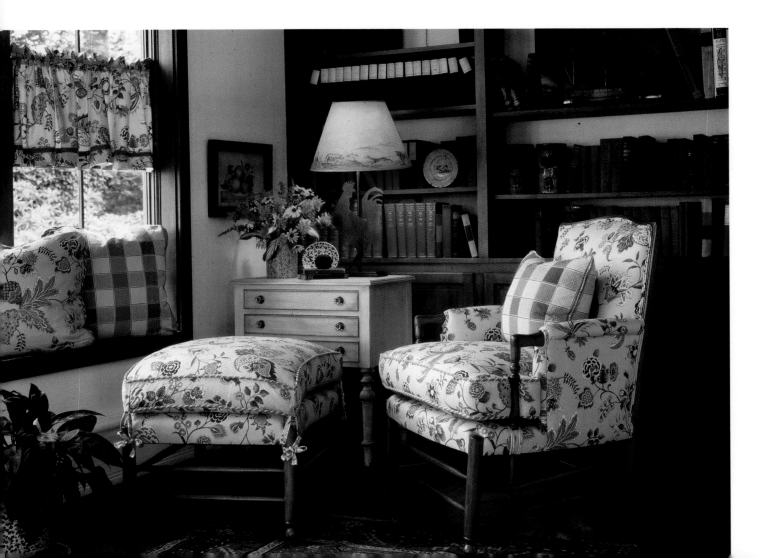

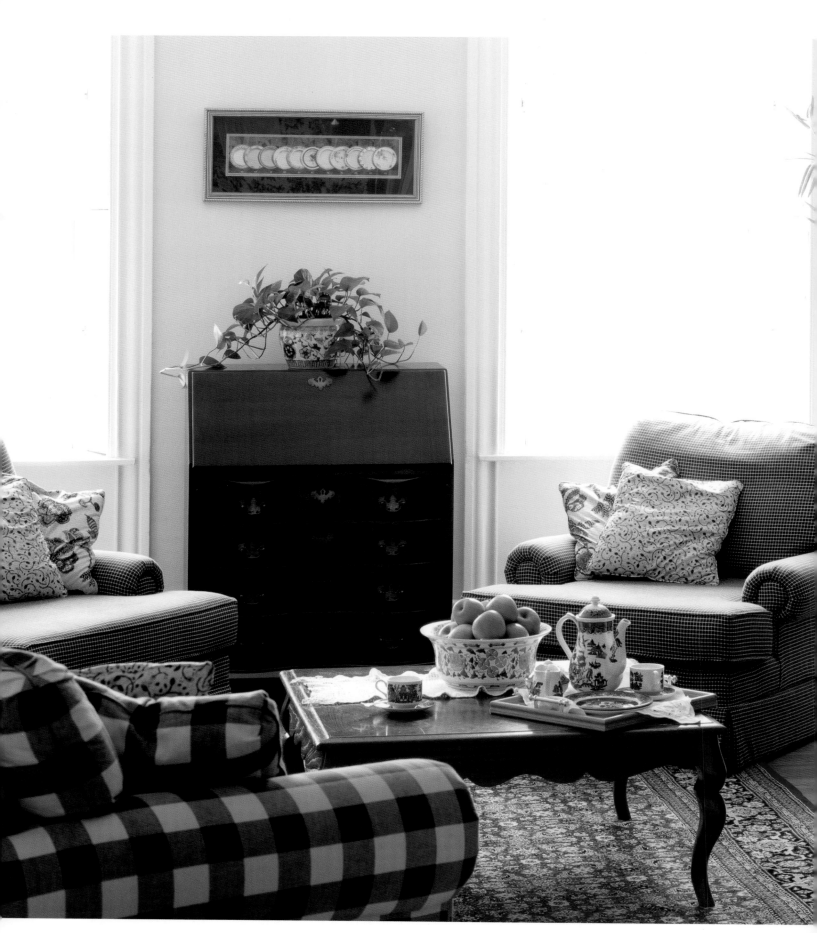

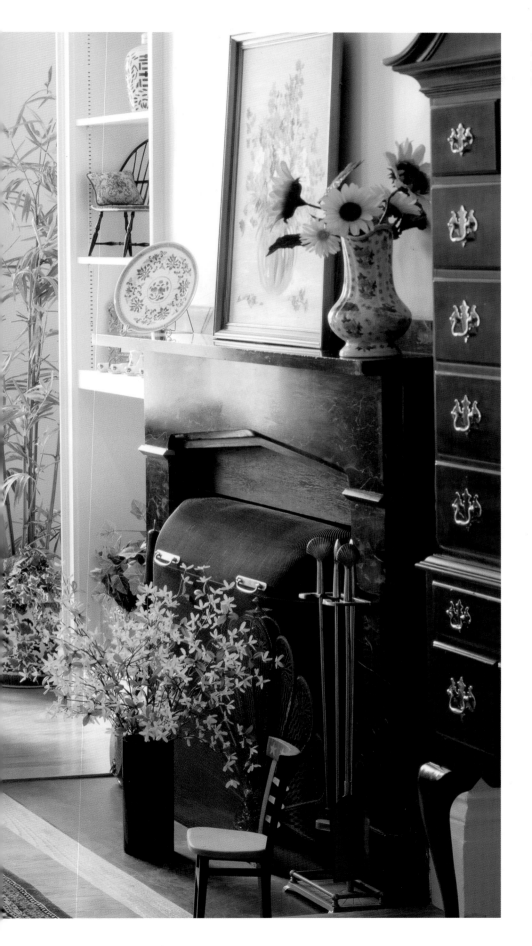

Unadorned windows make small living rooms seem larger, as do light wall colors in pale, buttery hues. Design: Constance Gallagher
Photo: Peter Jaquith

# Living Room
## *details*

*Fireplaces are living room focal points, so dress up yours with details that set the tone for the rest of the room. When planning furnishings, keep in mind practical needs such as storage. In you selection of patterns and fabrics, though, express the exuberant side of your decorating imagination.*

*Light Sources*

In country living rooms, lamps and lampshades range from quirky to quaint. Adapted from bottles, shaped into lighthouses, or following a Western motif, they provide lighting for cozy reading corners (below). Photo of lighthouse lamp courtesy of Crate & Barrel

*Exhibition Space*

A fireplace with its mantel is the perfect showcase to display a theme for a room while expressing personal interests, such as hunting, fishing, or sailing (below).
Photo of fireplace screen by Ron Maier, courtesy of New West

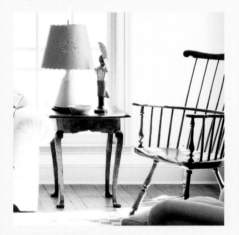

*Stylish Storage*

Because today's country living rooms are multi-purpose, look for furniture that serves more than one function. A blanket chest, for instance, both serves as a coffee table and provides storage for games or craft supplies (below).

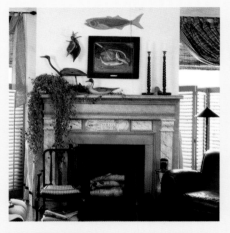

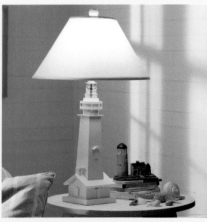

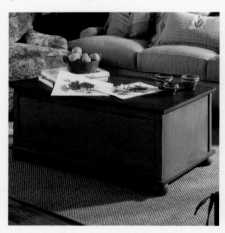

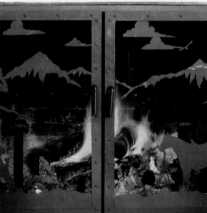

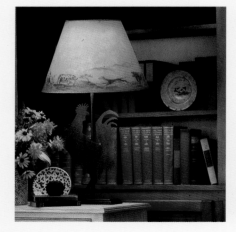

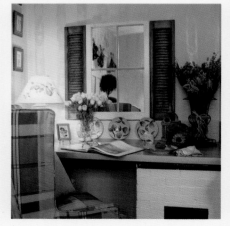

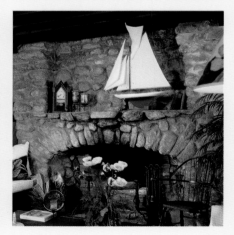

*Country Patterns*

Cover sofas and chairs in checks, chintz, and quilt patterns for an instant country look (below).

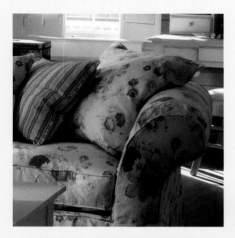

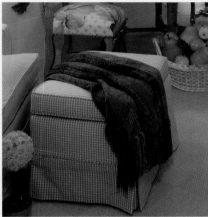

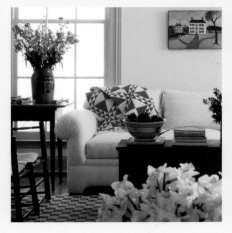

*Second Time Around*

Old and worn furniture, fun to search for and inexpensive to buy, adds weathered charm to country living rooms (below).

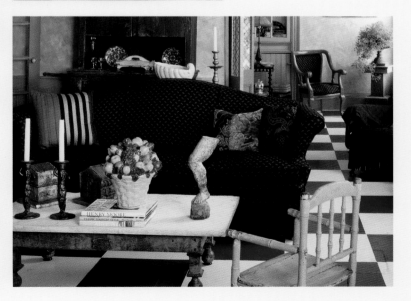

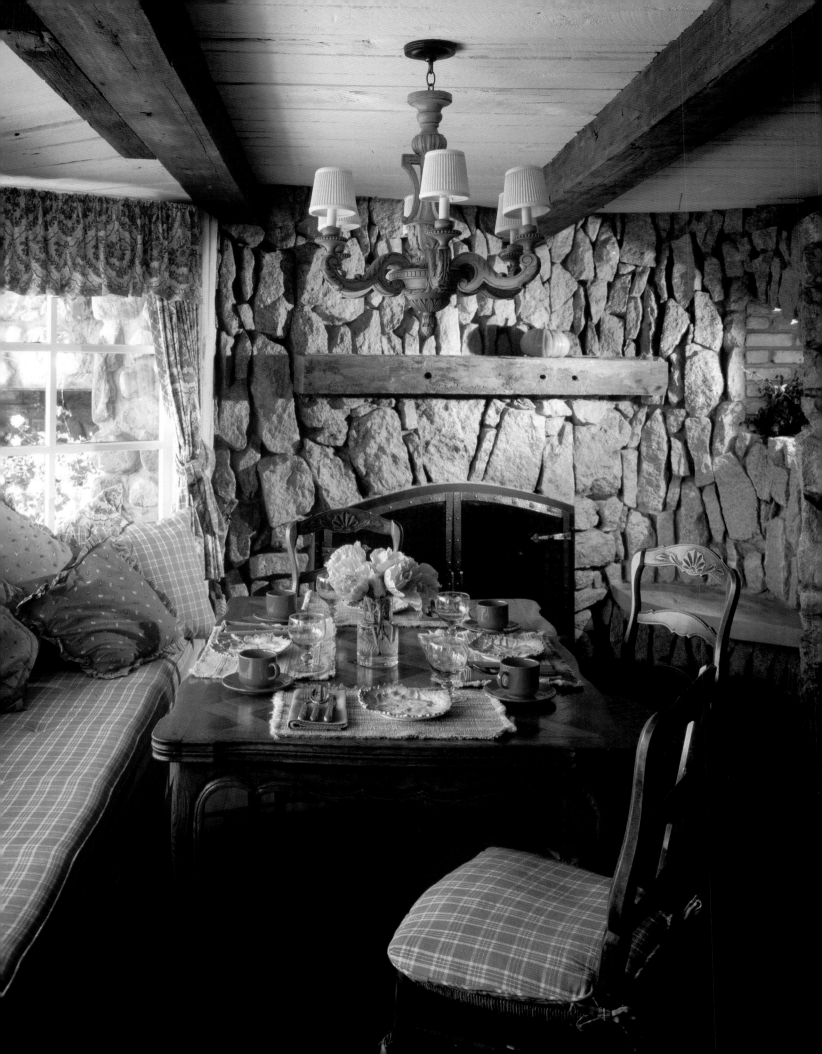

# *Country* Dining Areas

*Throughout the ages, sharing a meal has created a bond between people. The root of the word companion means "with bread," and the spirit of companionship does indeed deepen among those who break bread at the same table.*

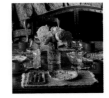 The connection between hospitable companionship and dining rooms is heightened in country homes because a welcoming ambience infuses the style in general. From compact breakfast nooks to expansive rooms geared to more formal repasts, country dining rooms offer family and friends easygoing comfort and a setting for relaxing conversation over good food.

Typically, the largest piece of dining room furniture —the table itself—sets the tone and becomes the room's centerpiece. Choose a table whose color and texture appeal to your sensibilities while fitting in with the architecture. A scratched and worn pine table is perfectly sympathetic with the log walls of an unfinished summer camp, but a Federal-era manor demands a more refined wood such as hand-rubbed cherry.

When it comes to selecting chairs, put comfort before aesthetics. Chair padding is always a plus; try loose cushions anchored with ties. Or consider dining on upholstered easy chairs or settees—seating options typically reserved for parlors but now making their way into more and more country dining rooms. Cane, rush, and other woven seats also afford more comfort than bare wood.

To make sure the dining room is not used merely for special occasions, design for function as well as comfort and aesthetics. Make sure all surfaces, including the floor, can be easily cleaned. In spacious rooms, provide storage and adjacent surfaces for serving by incorporating buffets or sideboards. In small spaces, tea carts or corner cabinets work well while occupying minimal space.

Functional considerations include lighting, which also has a profound impact on aesthetics. No matter which style you choose—farmhouse, French country, Western ranch, or new country—multi-layered lighting design can transform a dining room. By selecting several options—a pendant light or chandelier hung over the table, decorative sconces on walls, and a mixed grouping of flickering candles on the tabletop—the room will take on a glow guaranteed to nurture true companionship.

**French country fabrics and polished furniture, juxtaposed with rugged fieldstone and rough-hewn beams, bring grace to this extraordinarily cozy dining area.** Photo: Balthazar Korab

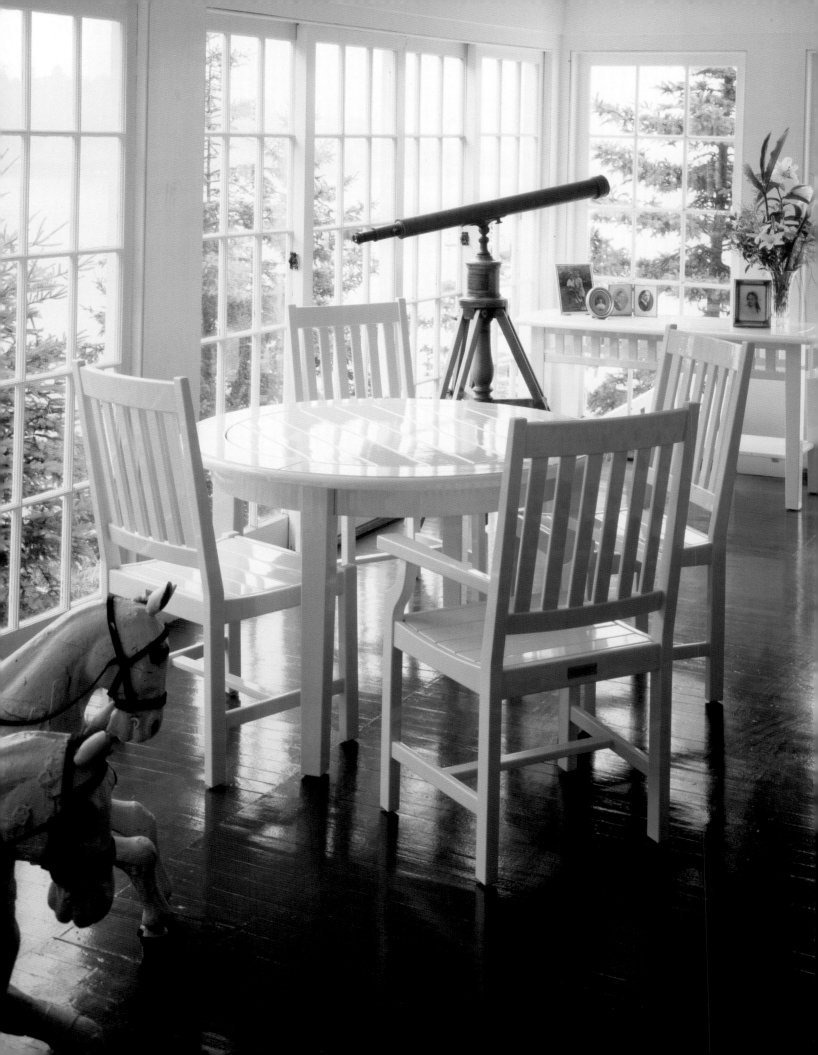

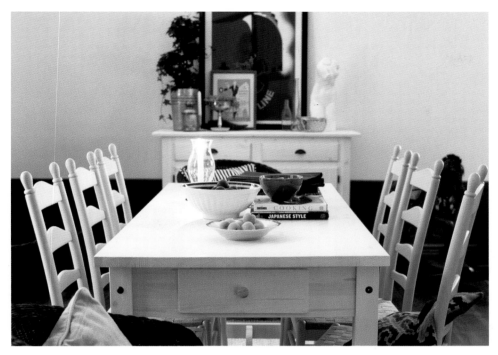

Ladder-back chairs and plain painted tables are country staples whose old style is refreshed when placed in a minimalist setting and juxtaposed with contemporary posters. Photo courtesy of IKEA

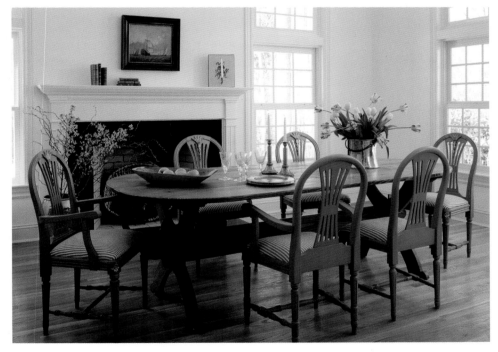

Trestle tables originated centuries ago as collapsible furniture for small dwellings whose rooms served multiple functions. Here the venerable style is mixed with elegant sheaf-back chairs from Sweden's Gustavian period. Photo courtesy of Country Swedish

New country style limits the number of striking design elements. A periwinkle blue floor grabs attention while also setting off the equally glossy white furniture. Photo courtesy of Weatherend Estate Furniture

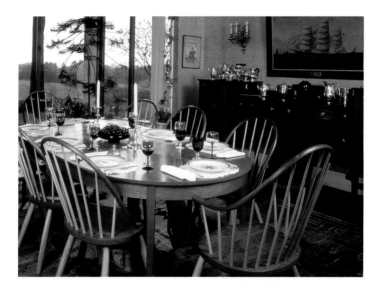

Traditional Windsor chairs, popular in England and her colonies in the eighteenth century, take a contemporary turn with straight spindles and cherry and ash materials. With its absence of carved detail and ornament, the dining room furniture typifies the new country genre. Photo: Paul Rocheleau, courtesy of Thos. Moser Cabinetmakers

Below: Dressed in cheerful yellow and plaid, this breakfast nook has a crisp, tailored look. The window treatment is a creative, clean-lined choice. Design: Nancy Fowler and Cynthia Francis, Interior Design Concepts Photo: Steve Vierra

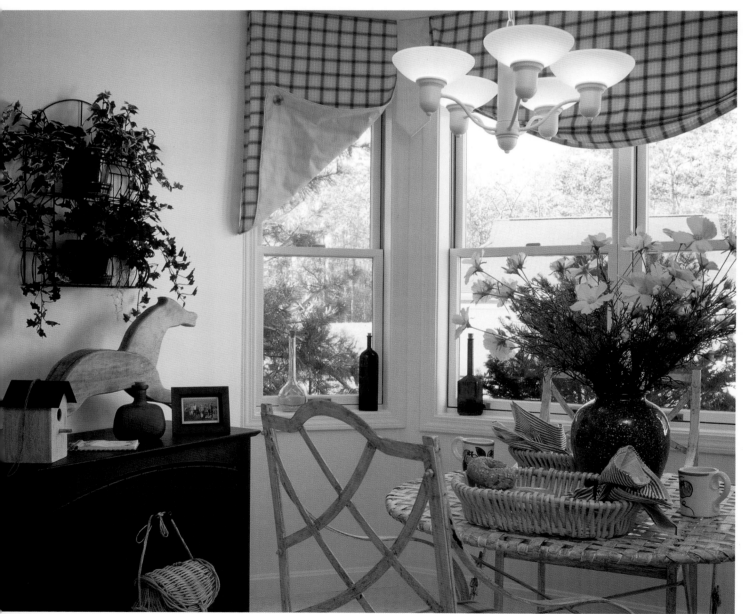

A striped wallpapered ceiling creates a sense of shelter under a canvas canopy. In response to the intensity of the stripes, other patterns are kept to a minimum. Design: David Barrett
Photo: Bill Rothschild

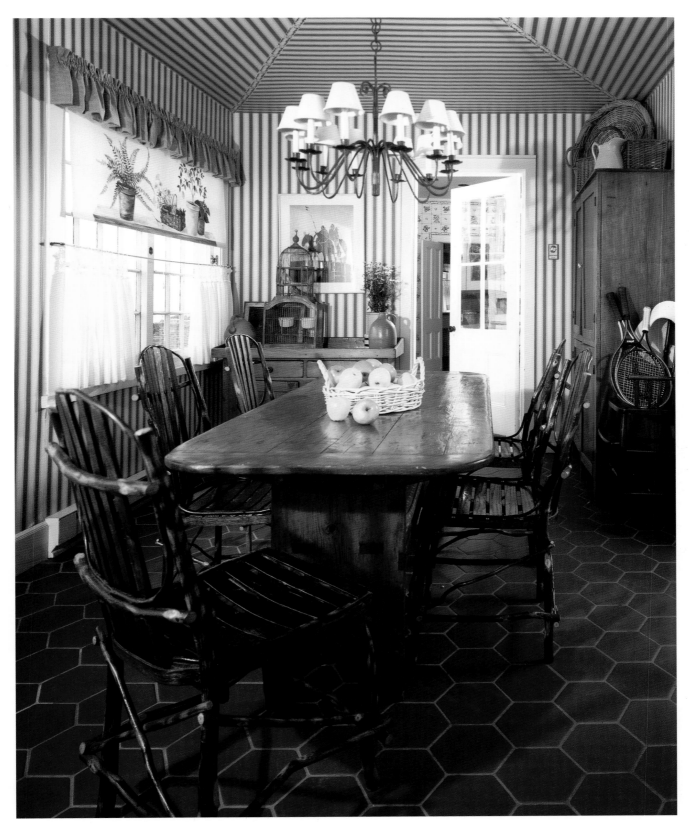

The sparseness of this dining room's decor no[t] only enlarges a tight space but also enhances the room's assets: antique furniture, a view of an orchard, and beautiful natural light. In smal[l] rooms, window seats save space and can acc[om]modate extra guests while doubling as a stora[ge] area for dining linens.
Photo: Eric Roth

Upholstered pieces are unexpected but delightful additions to a dining room. The camelback sofa invites postprandial lounging around the table.
Design: Susan Zises Green; Photo: Eric Roth

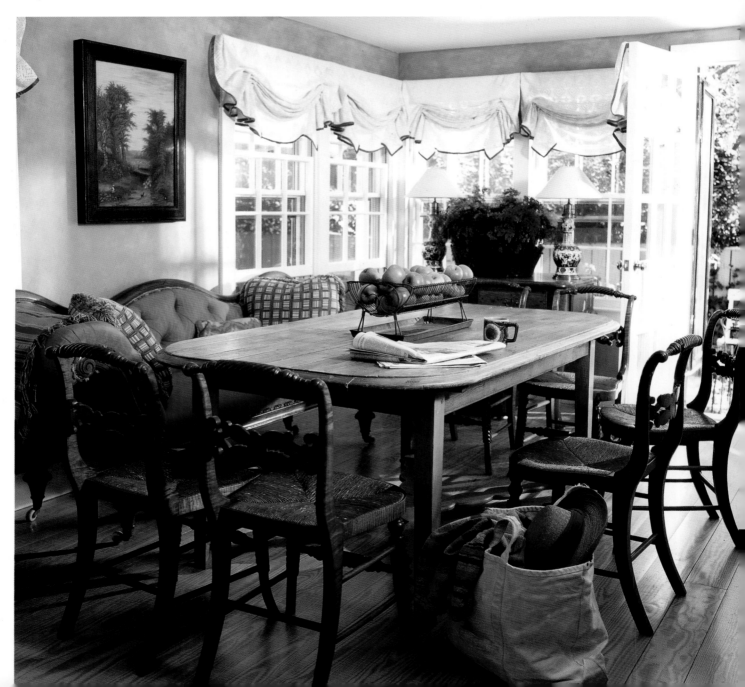

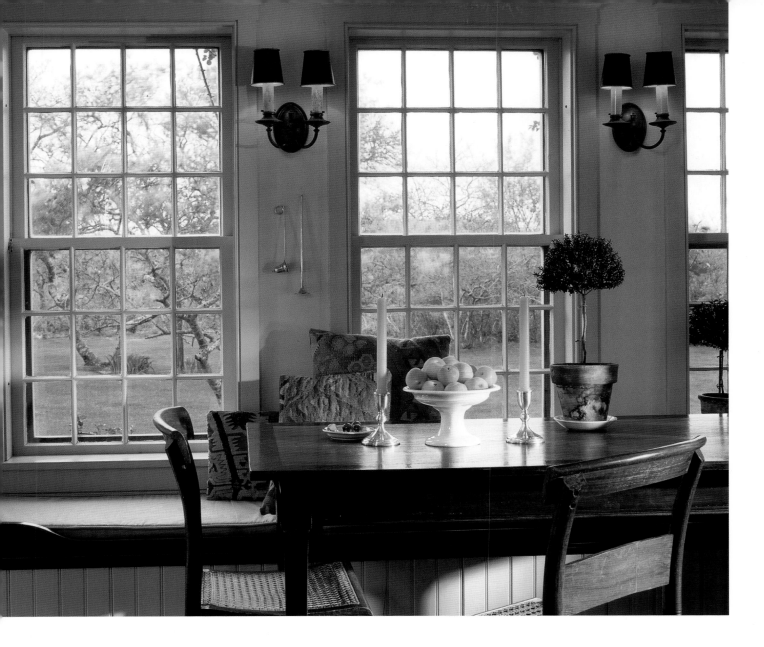

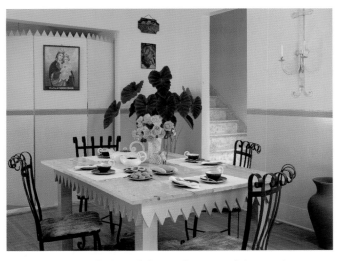

The unorthodox use of color and shape in this unique dining room jazz up new country style with Southern California flair. The whimsical attitude common to such rooms comes through in the curled-back iron chairs and zigzag edge of the table and folding screen. Design: Annie Kelly; Photo: Tim Street-Porter

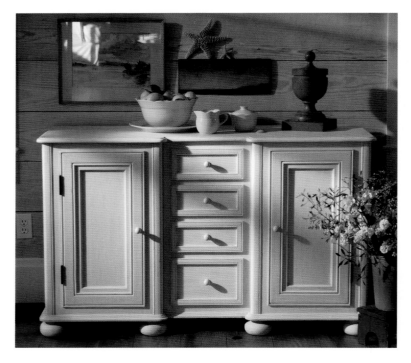

Give a simple dining room an appealing sea-washed aesthetic with bleached wooden walls, a white table, and natural pine chairs with canvas pads. The woven cotton rug adds a splash of color, as do the objects on and near the buffet.

Photos courtesy of Crate and Barrel

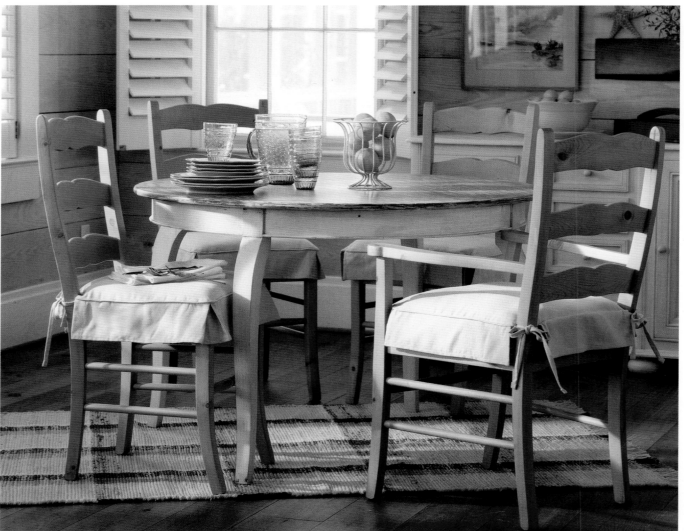

Below: New country interiors, with their Spartan aesthetic, walk a fine line between contemporary and traditional. Incorporate modern elements, such as the artwork, light fixture, and window treatment in this eating area, with natural materials, such as the rush in baskets and chair seats and the wood used in furniture, cabinetry, and flooring. Design: Tom Sokel
Photo: Steve Vierra

Next pages: A variety of painted chairs, tables, and side pieces illustrates the range of Swedish country style. The overall effect is light and airy, with classic European designs given a pastoral touch by paint and simplified lines.
Photo courtesy of Country Swedish

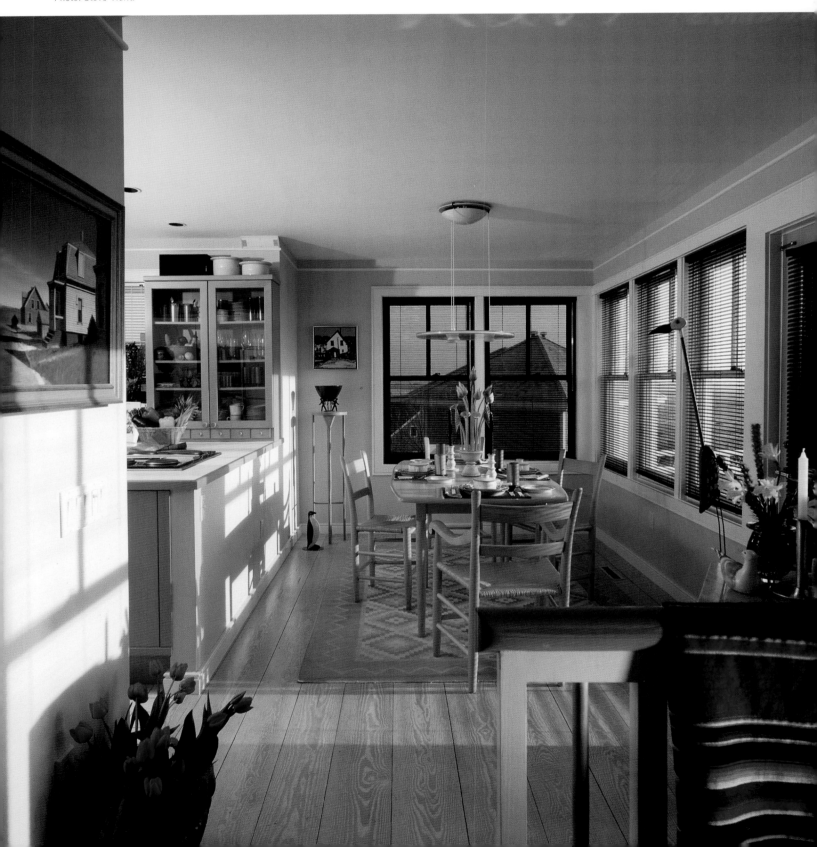

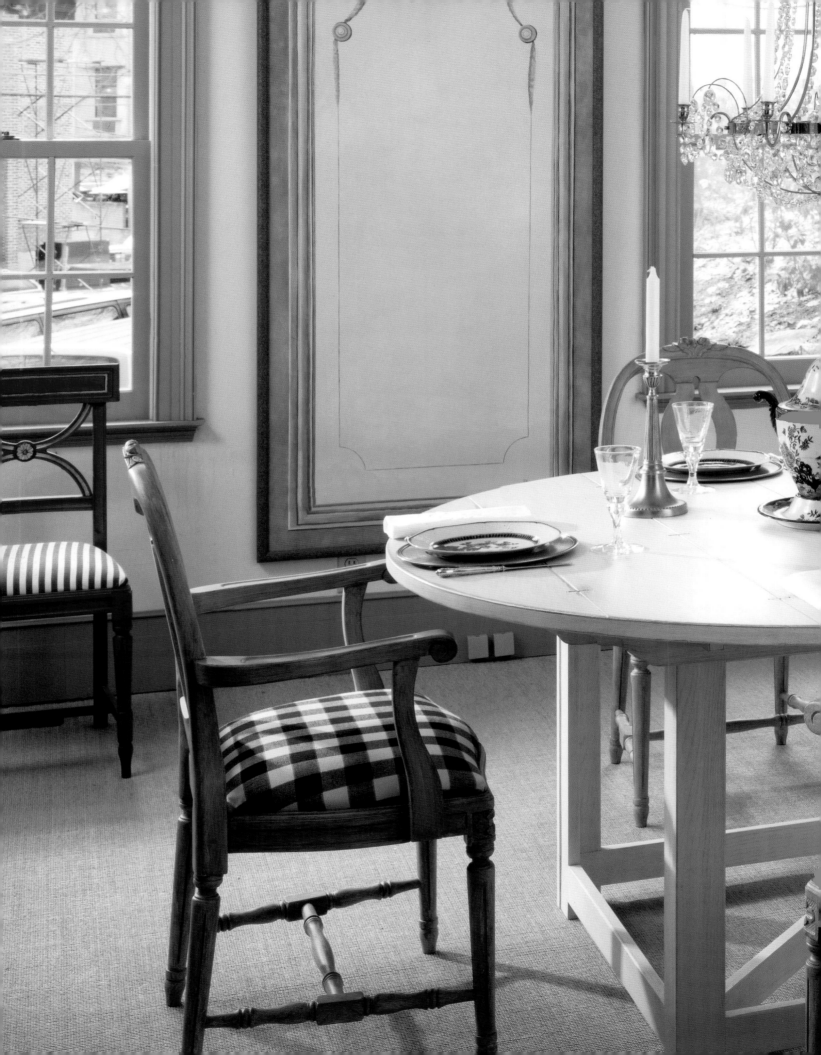

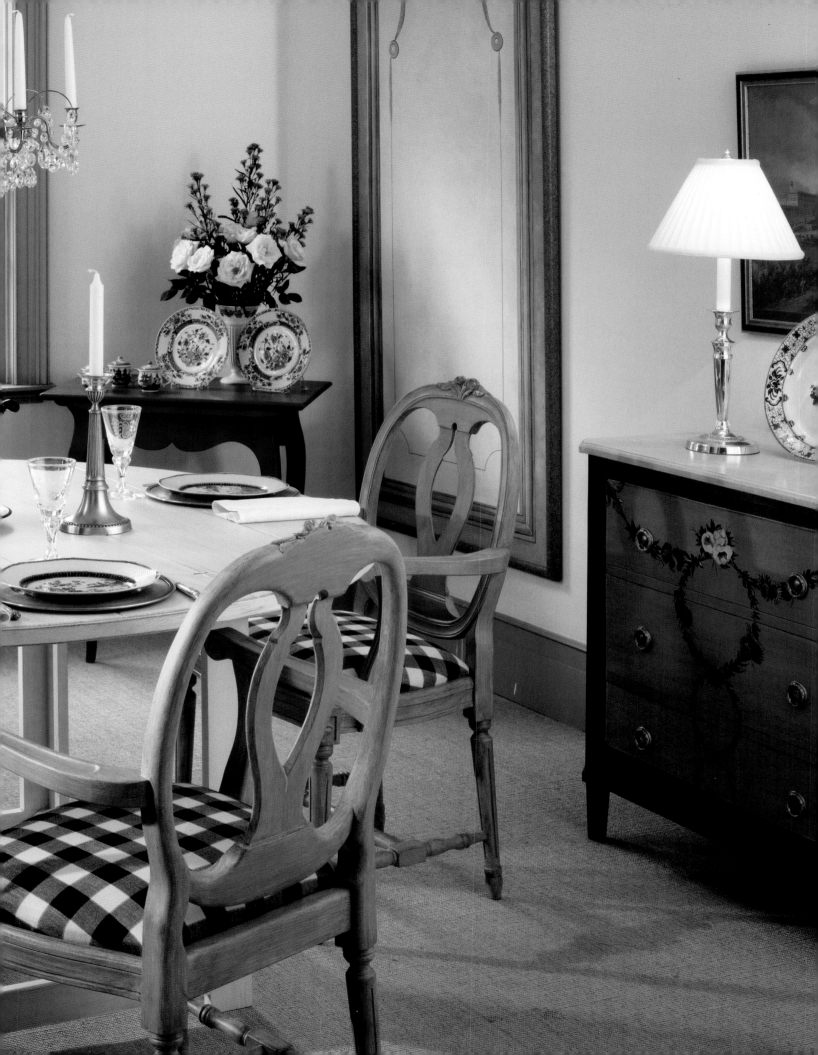

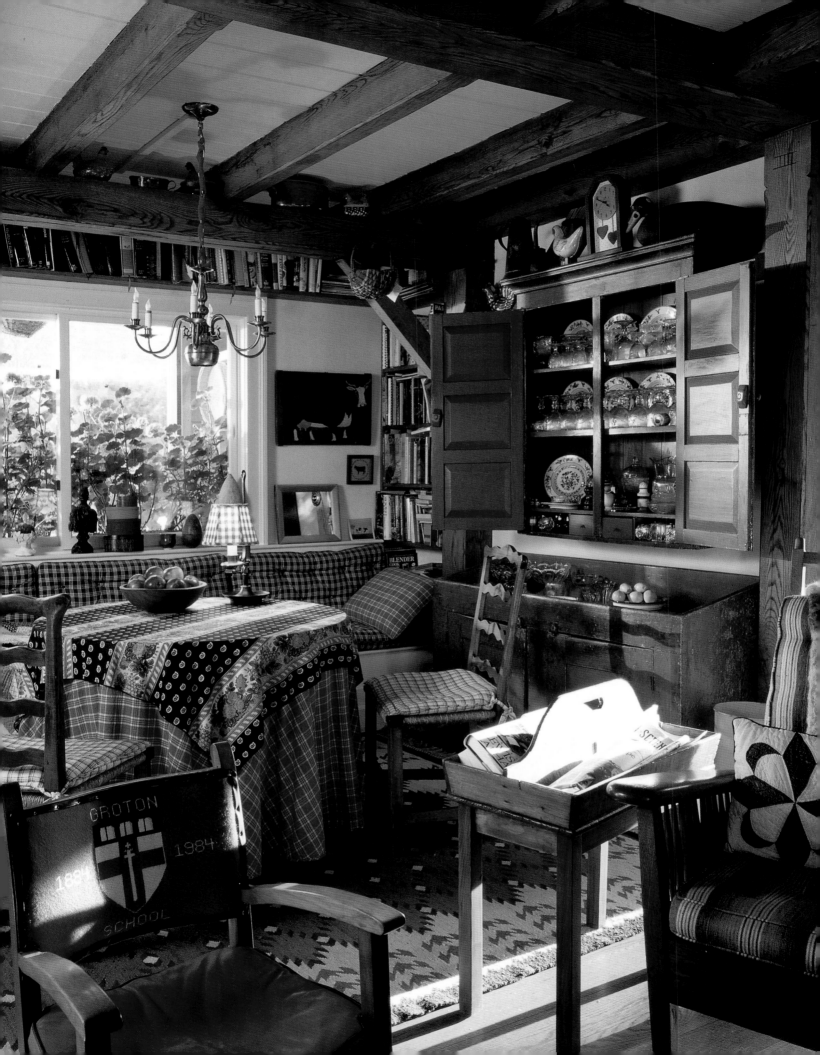

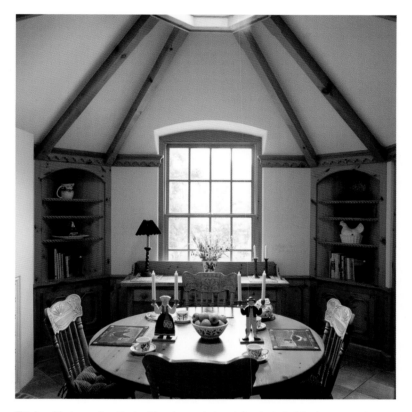

This breakfast room has the traditional carved pine styling typical of the homeowner's native Austria. A lofty conical ceiling creates an airy ambience, with natural illumination from the skylight bathing the dining table and chairs.
Design: Austin Patterson Disston Architects; Photo: Adrianne dePolo

An exuberant use of textiles adds to the comfortable look of this dining nook bordering a family room. Although the fabric patterns vary, blues, reds, and whites weave throughout the room to create a unified design. Photo: Eric Roth

Wrought-iron chairs and a sunny yellow palette are reminiscent of al fresco dining on a summer patio, bringing freshness indoors. Centerpieces need not be elaborate; here, lemons piled in a pedestal bowl are a lovely decorative touch. Design: Leslie Fetherston Tuttle, Tuttle-Bradley Photo: Peter Jaquith

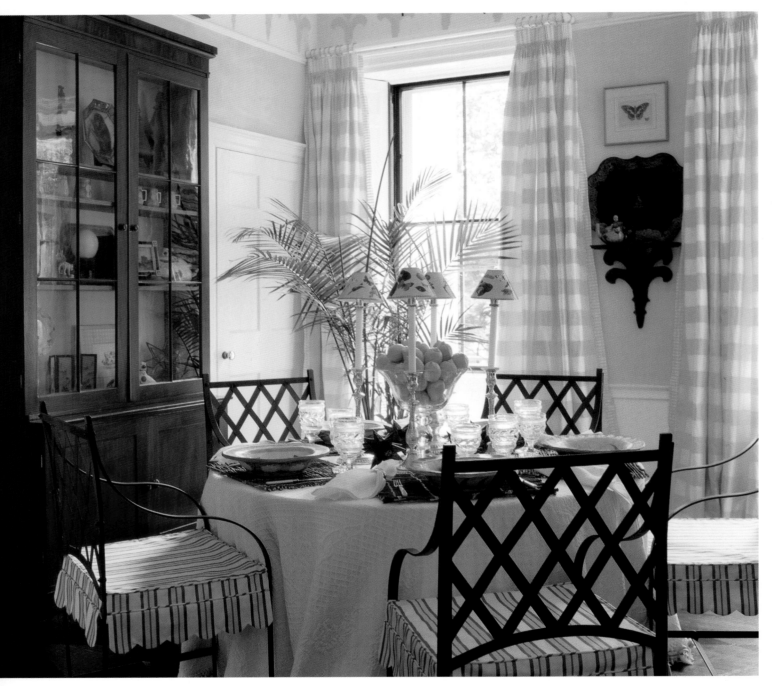

Opposite: White walls and woodwork provide a bright, clean backdrop for the varied textures of rustic furnishings. The chandelier's elk-horn styling, the table's knotty wooden surface, and the chairs' leather and willow backs all gain textural punch against solid white. Design: Barbara Barry; Photo: Tim Street-Porter

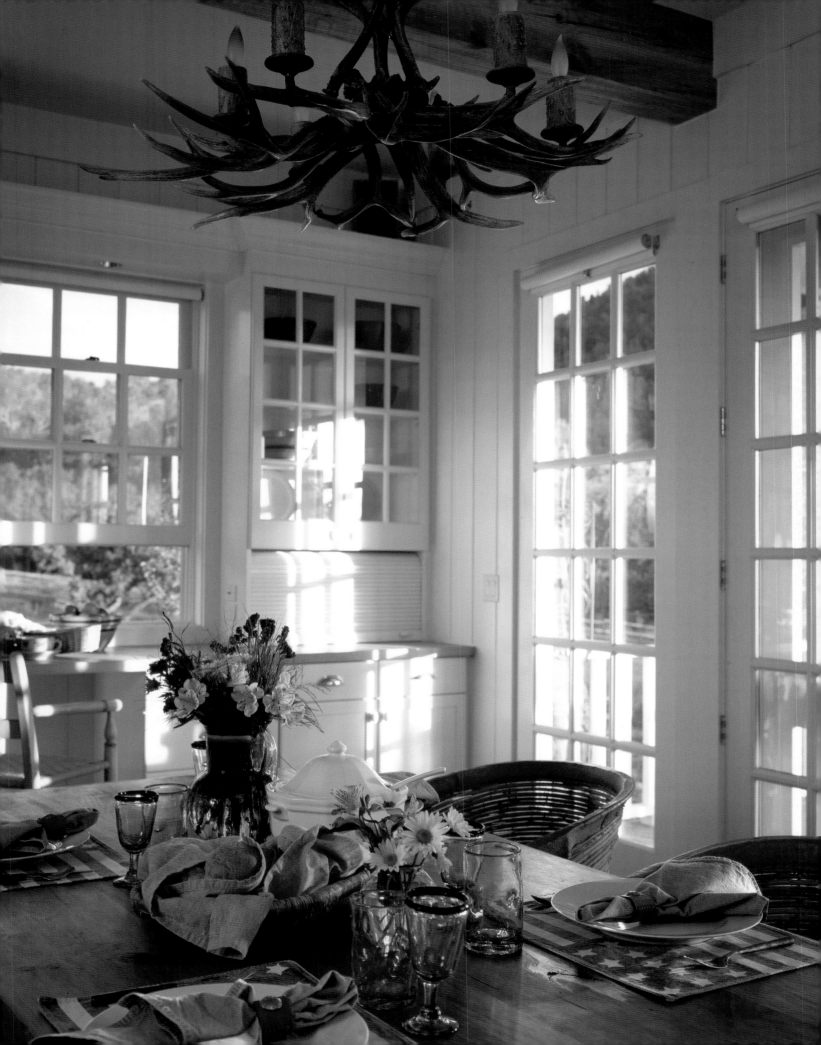

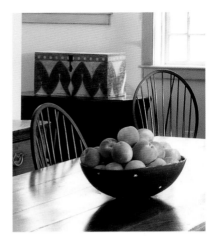

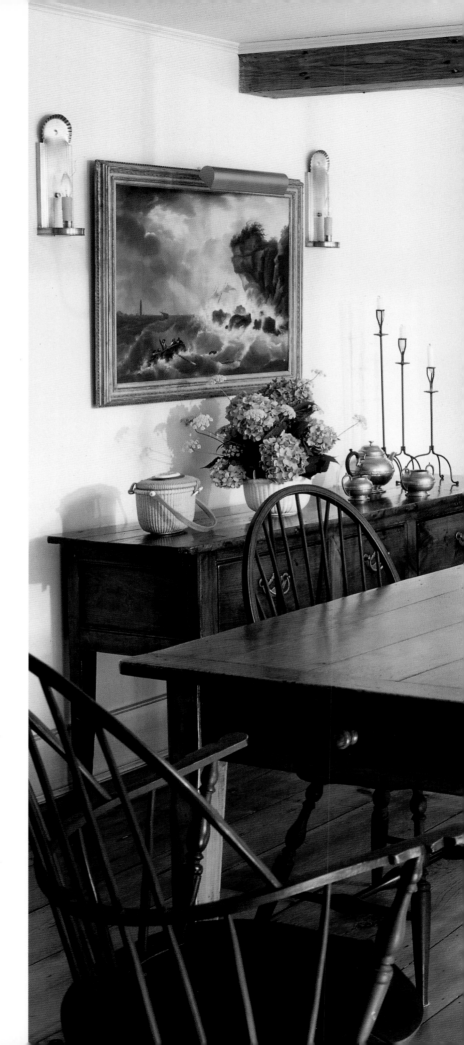

The best rustic interiors, such as this dining room on Nantucket Island, incorporate local flavor. In this setting, nautical paintings are appropriate, as is the sideboard's Nantucket lightship basket, an item made by old-time sailors to pass the time at sea. Design: Kevin and Joanne Paulsen; Photo: Eric Roth

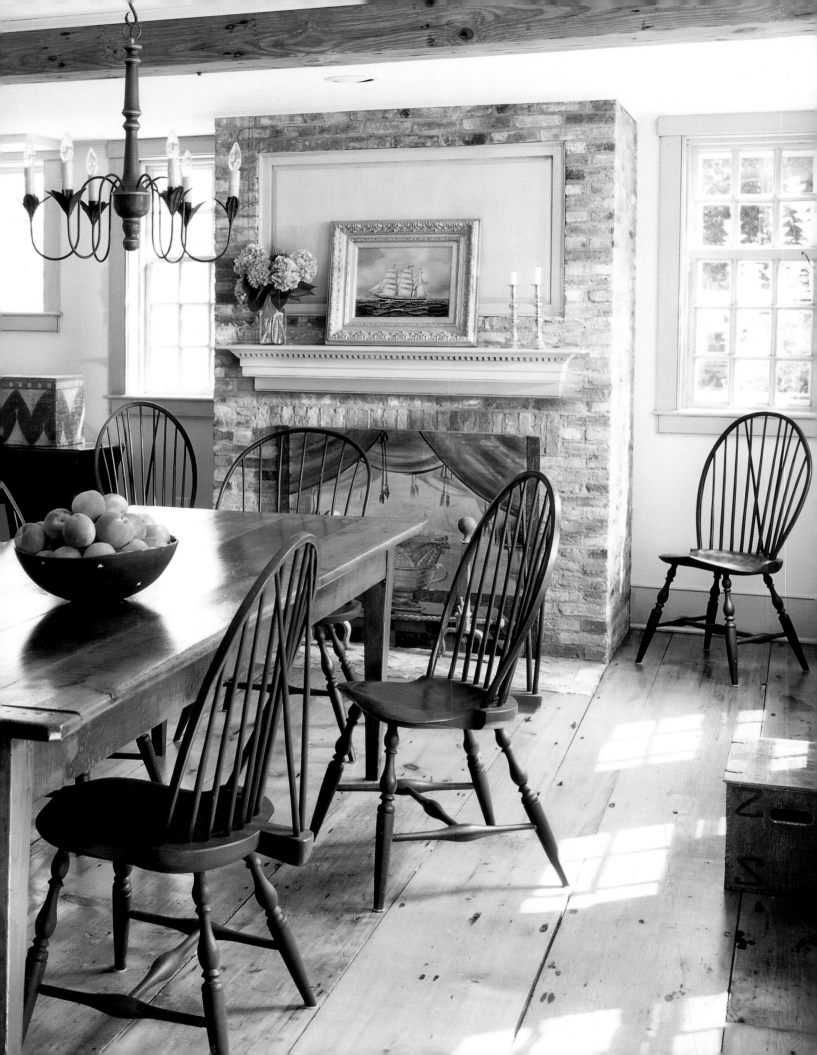

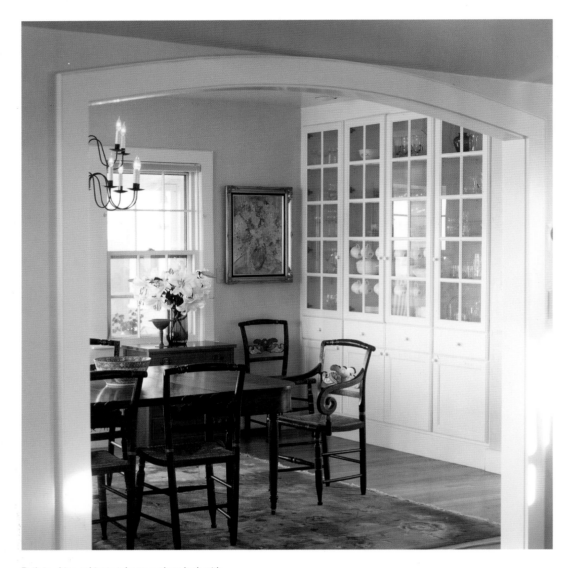

Built-in china cabinets take on a clean look with simple mullion glass doors and minimal moldings. During the daytime, accordion shades tuck neatly against the top window frame, leaving the spare aesthetic intact.

Design: Kalman Construction; Photo: Eric Roth

Striped walls bring energy to this small dining area. Old chairs—one with dusty-rose upholstery and the other with painted wood worn to a soft patina—subdue the effect. Design: Annie Kelly Photo: Tim Street-Porter

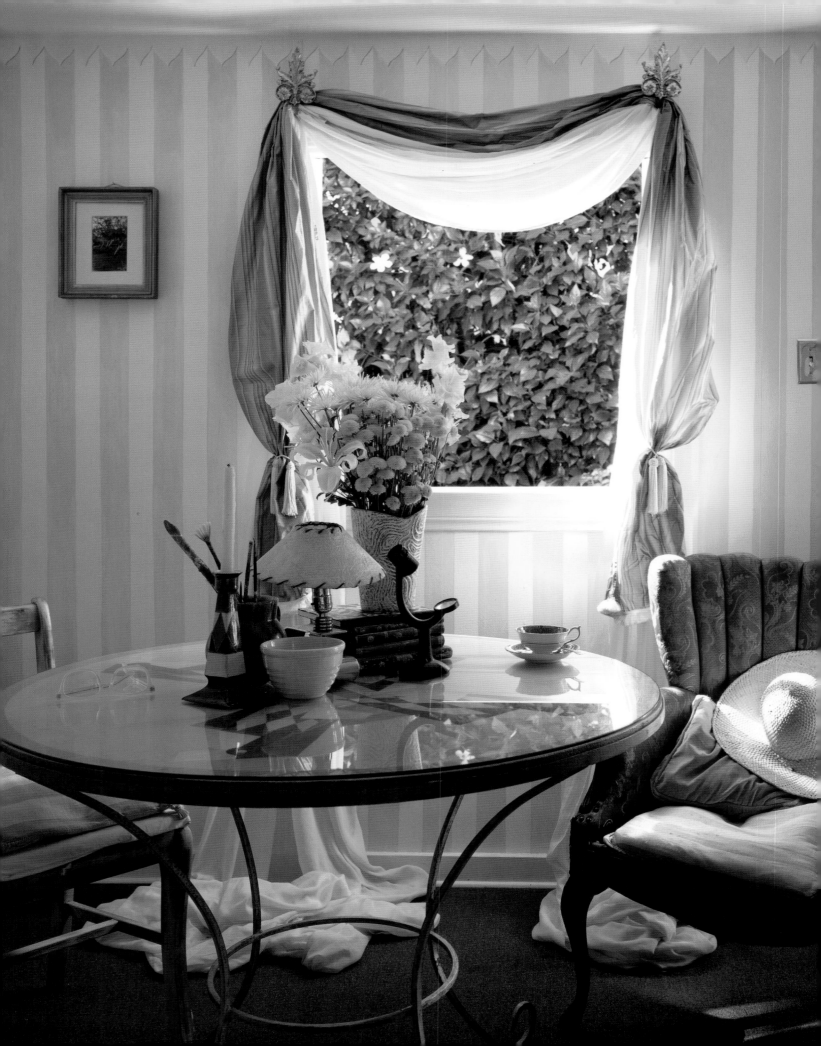

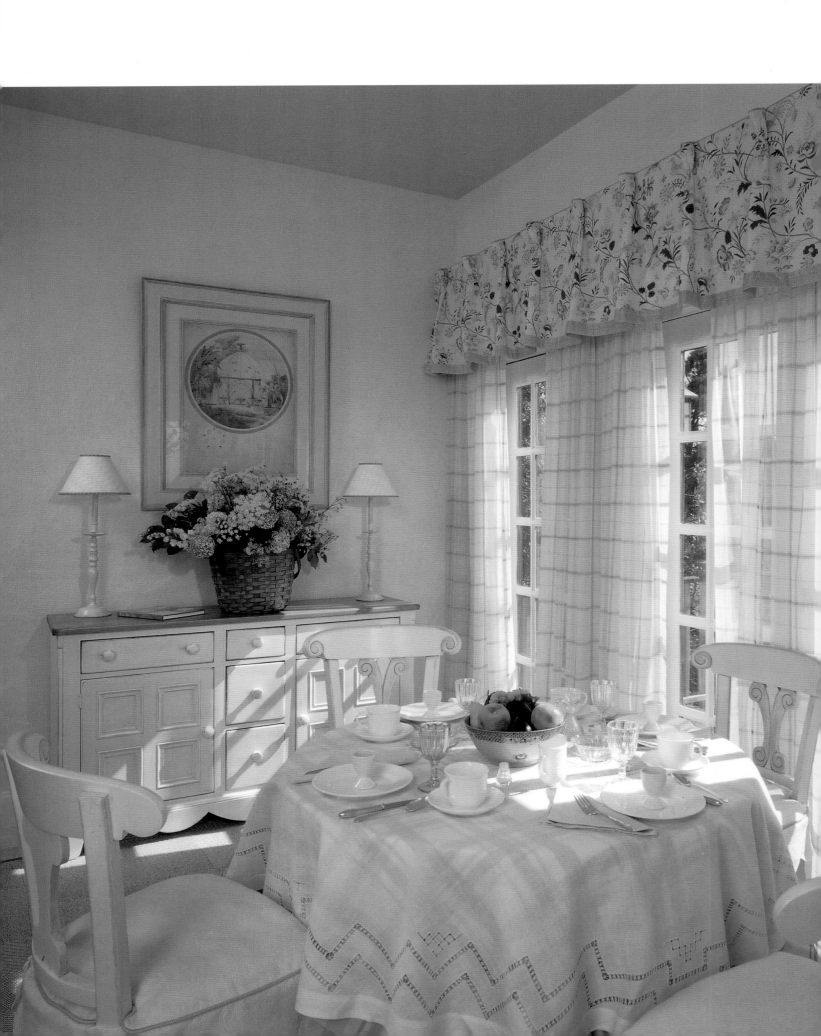

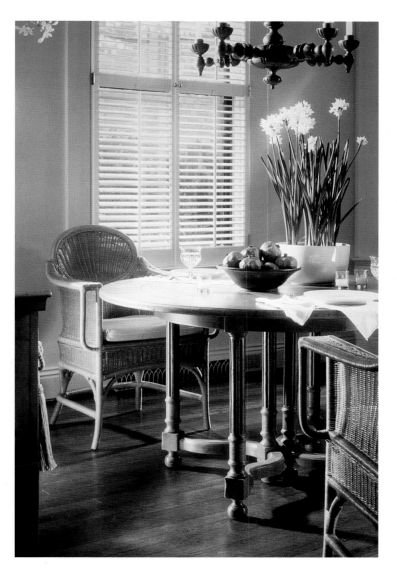

Wickerwork, as in the chairs' interlaced twigs, brings natural earthiness to any room. Fragrant paperwhite narcissus growing in a bowl are another wonderful connection to nature in this country dining room. Photo: Kenton Robertson, courtesy of Milling Road

The painted chairs and sideboard, pale palette, and pristine aesthetic create a Swedish country look. Design: Manijeh M. Emery, M. M. Interiors Photo: Steve Vierra

Next pages: Wheat-back chairs and a massive painted china cabinet filled with majolica ware lend European country styling to this pretty dining room. With a nod to whimsy, the sisal carpet is casually strewn with painted leaves.
Design: Jeanne Leonard; Photo: Bill Rothschild

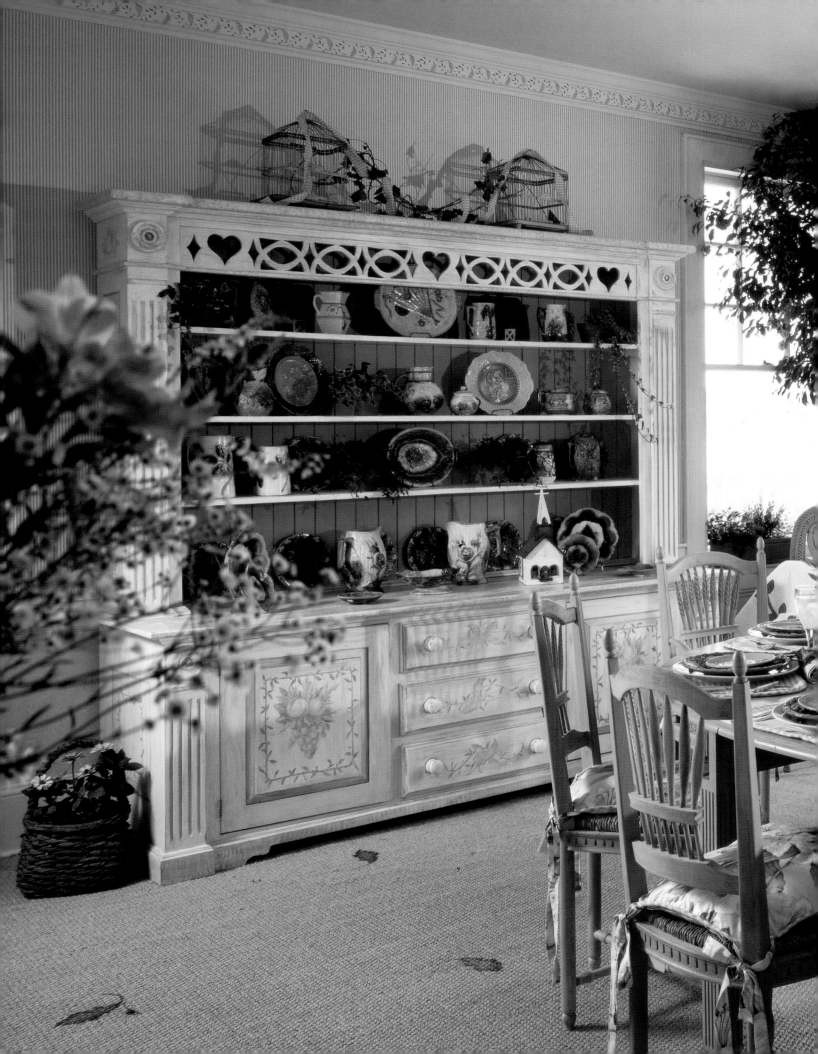

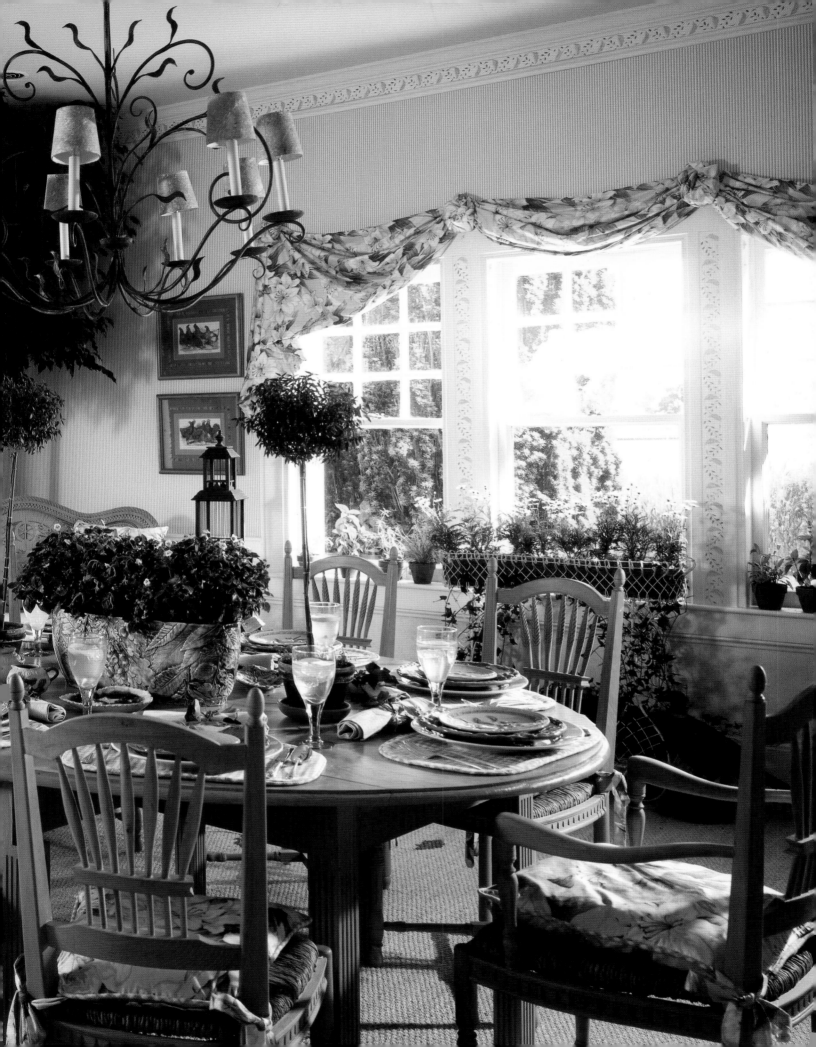

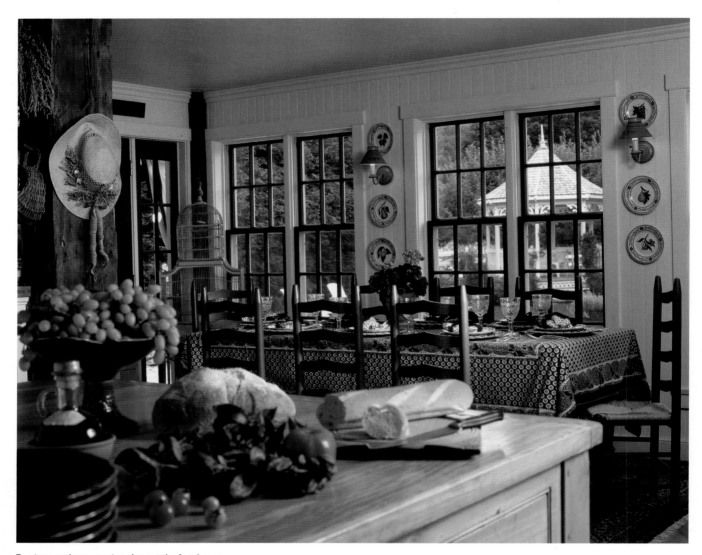

Furniture and accessories play out the farmhouse theme beautifully, while the basic architectural materials—exposed timbers and white bead-board paneling—provide an excellent design foundation. Leaving the windows unadorned and painting the sashes and mullions green gives them decorative emphasis and carries the outdoors in.
Design: Lillian Bogossian and Vivian Weil, Decorative Interiors; Photo: Steve Vierra

With an easy-to-wipe tabletop and painted checkerboard hardwood floor, this breakfast room is low maintenance for day-to-day use.
Design: Austin Patterson Disston Architects
Photo: Adrianne dePolo

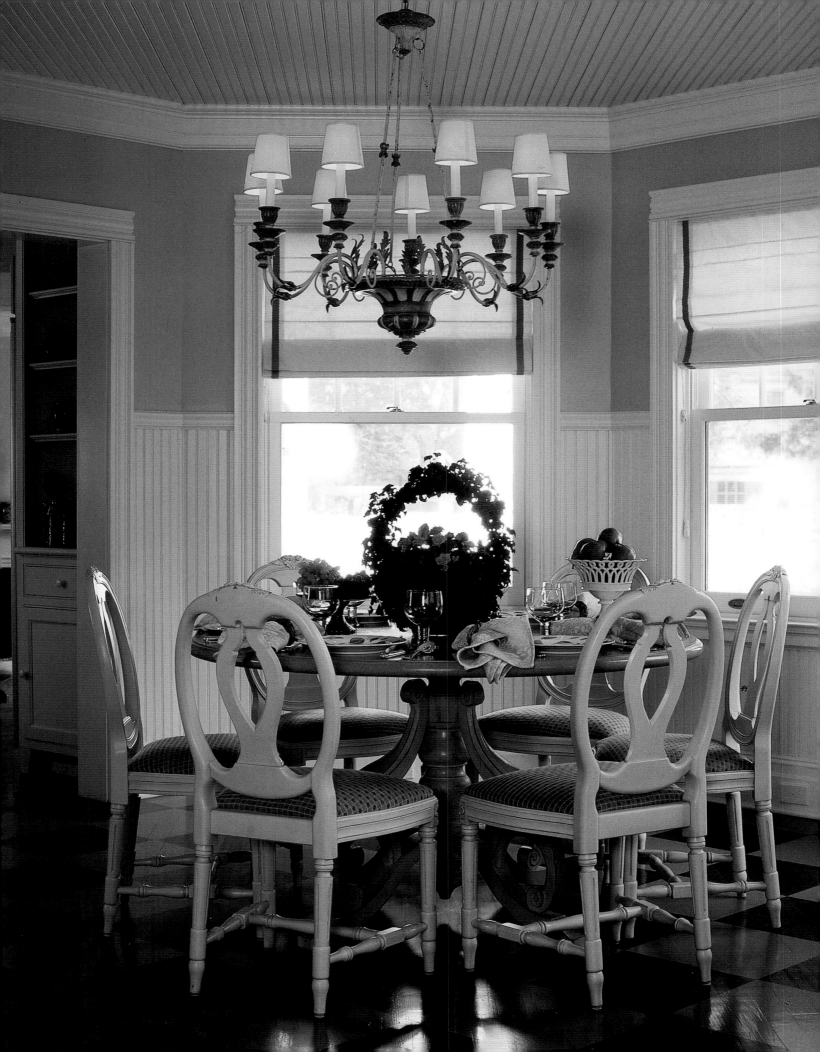

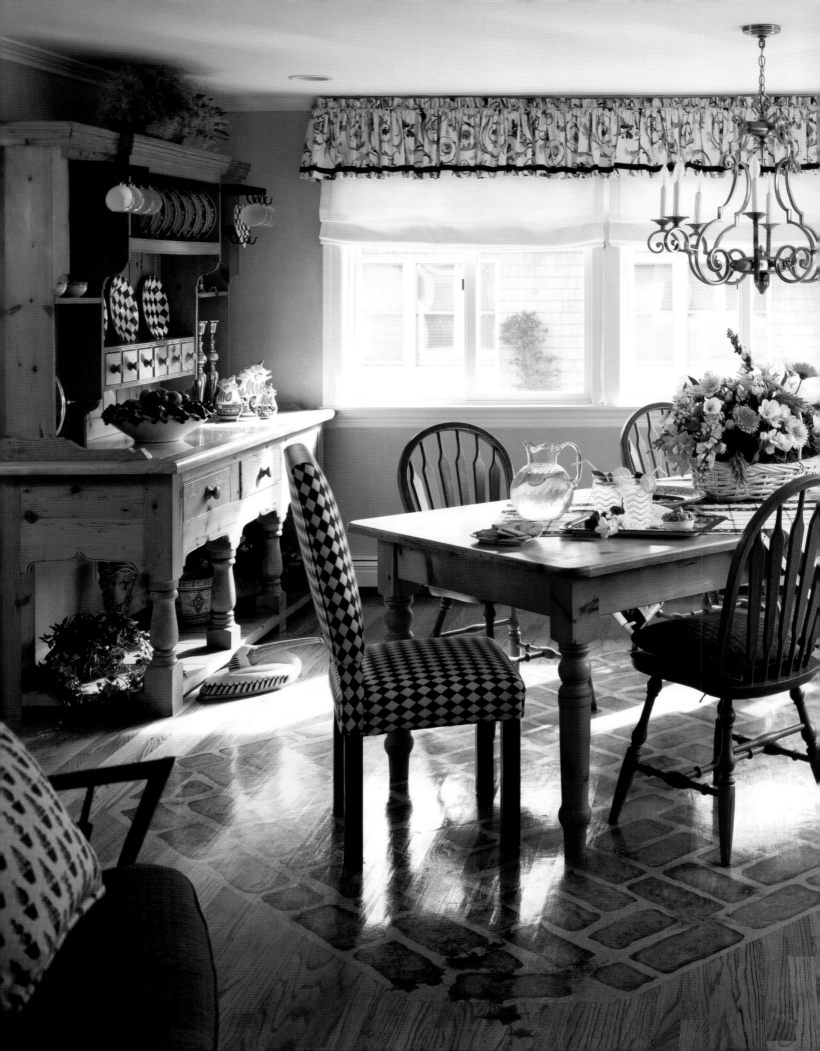

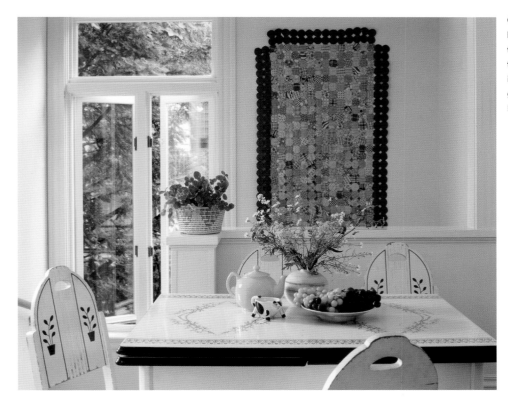

Country-style furniture, used sparingly, adds homespun flavor to this contemporary architectural space, with a blue-on-white enamel-top table and chairs next to a wall hanging made in the style of a yo-yo quilt, out of checked, gingham, and plaid fabric scraps.
Photo: Eric Roth

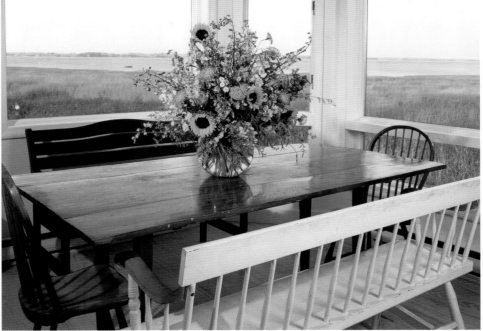

In new country rooms, bare windows let the outside in, so landscape views become part of the decor. A casual mix of benches and chairs echoes the salt marsh, an environment whose few elements are beautiful in their unaffected simplicity. Photo: Eric Roth

A sturdy pine hutch is attractive and highly functional for storage and as an adjunct serving area. Displayed porcelain coordinates with the room's palette, and the upholstered dining chair perfectly matches the dishes' diamond pattern.
Design: Teri Seidman; Photo: Bill Rothschild

# Dining Area
## details

*Detail your dining room with a multi-layered lighting scheme and displays of china and glassware. Comfortable seating deserves special consideration, too, since lingering over meals is integral to the country way of life.*

*Quick-Change Act*

**Chair pads with ties can be changed with the seasons to create a completely new look (below).** Photos courtesy of Crate and Barrel

*Dining with Ease*

**Incorporate comfortable upholstered seating such as wing-back chairs or even a curvaceous sofa to encourage leisurely family-style dining (below).**

Bottom photo design: Alexis Ryan

Photo: Bill Rothschild

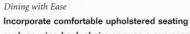

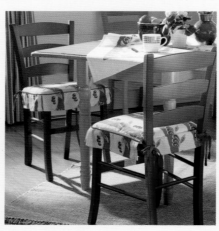

*China Fair*

**Make porcelain and glassware part of the decor by displaying it in a hutch or china cabinet. In tight rooms, a hanging cabinet or corner hutch is a great space-saving option (below).**

Bottom photo design: Maggie Cohen

Photo: Bill Rothschild

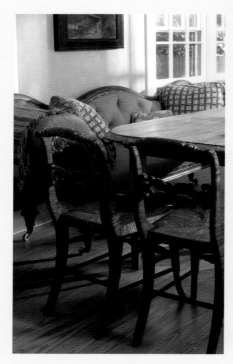

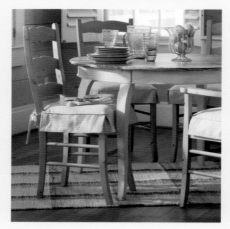

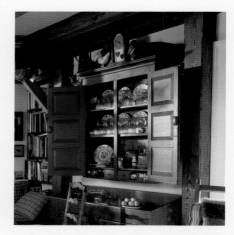

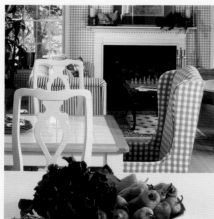

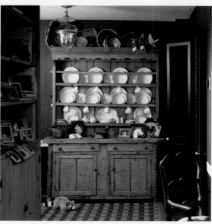

*Built-In Comfort*

**Banquette seating with colorful cushions offers country panache and provides additional space for guests in small dining areas (below).**

Top photo design: Brett Nestler
Photo: Bill Rothschild

*Shedding Light*

**Light a country dining room with traditional wood and wrought-iron chandeliers. Hang wall sconces to shed light on a wall hanging or china collection. Arrange a grouping of glowing candles for one of the least expensive and most effective ways to bring instant warmth to country dining rooms (below).** Top photo design: Nancy Goslee Power; Photo: Tim Street-Porter

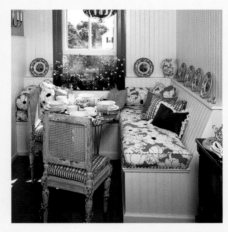

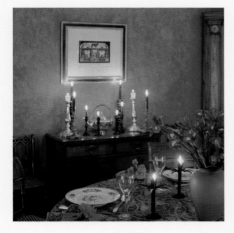

*Plant Life*

**Continue the garden indoors by lining the window with herbs in clay pots or a luxuriant collection of wild flowers and annuals (below).**

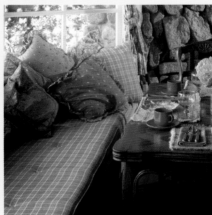

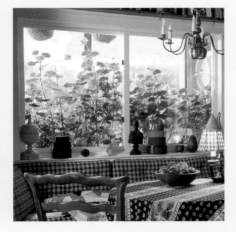

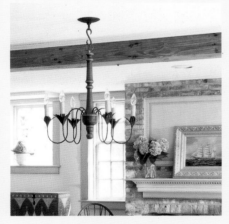

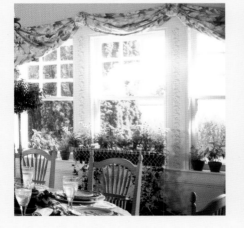

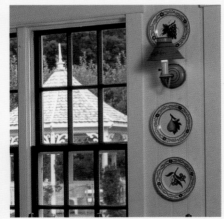

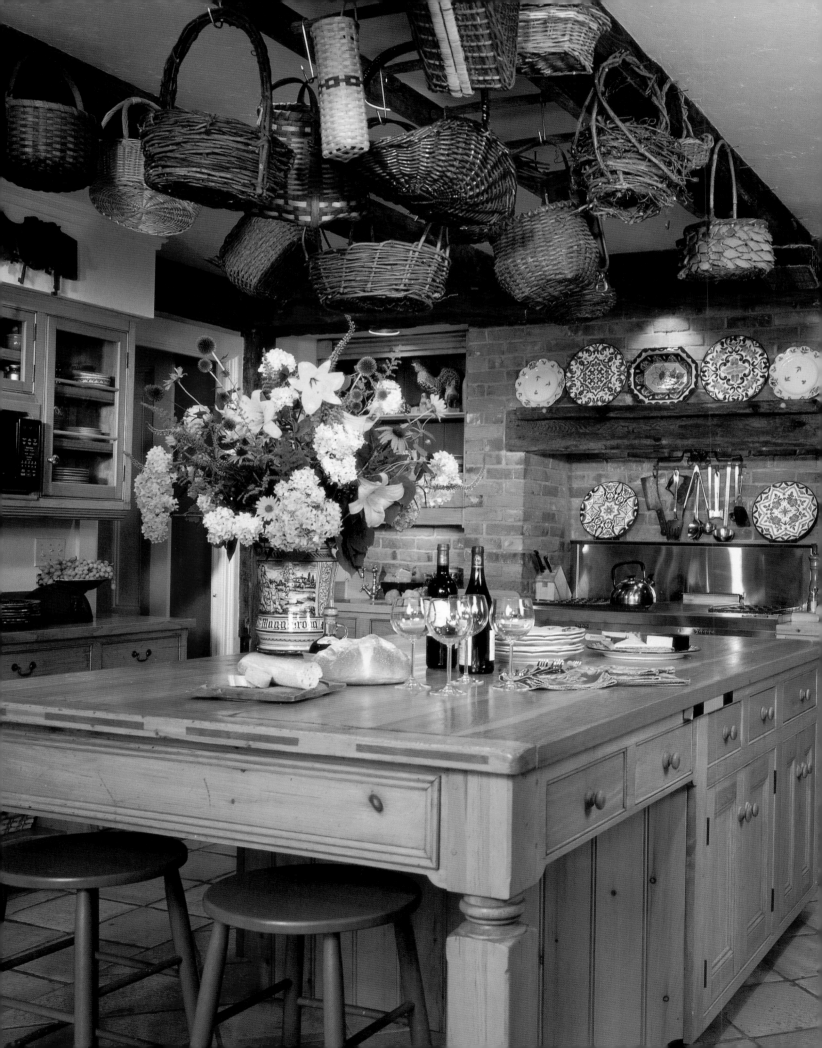

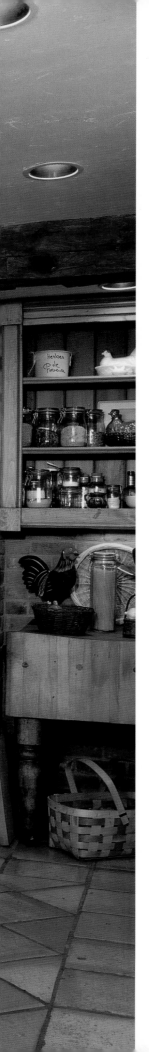

# *Country* Kitchens

*Country style was made for kitchens. It seems only natural to apply this unaffected, basic design approach to the room that satisfies one of the most basic human needs—the need to eat.*

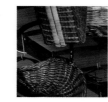

Unfortunately, the link is so obvious that country kitchens have almost become a cliché in recent decades. But opportunities for fresh approaches abound. As cooks discover easy-to-prepare cuisine, their kitchens are pared down and made less fussy.

Good kitchen design should play with the senses, much as a medley of red, green, and yellow peppers delights the eye or the aroma of fresh pesto tantalizes the nose. With those images in mind, think about the sensory interest of a homespun rag rug's nubby texture, a cabinet washed in faded moss green, the shape of a graceful wooden bowl, the dance of light on gleaming hand-painted tiles, the familiar pattern of checked tablecloths. Design options for country kitchens are endless, so select as judiciously as you would a ripe summer tomato.

Practical considerations are every bit as important as aesthetics. Remember that the kitchen is

a workshop. The cook's craft requires countertops and ample storage. The stove, refrigerator, and sink should be in handy proximity to one another, ideally an equal distance apart in what is known as the work triangle. Task areas such as the cooktop and cutting surfaces must be well lit. And because a country kitchen is an irresistible gathering place, ambient lighting should glow on everyone drawn to the room.

While fitted kitchens with built-in cabinetry have dominated the world of kitchen design since the 1960s, many people now see the appeal of freestanding kitchen furniture. Long rows of identical cabinets can become boring; try a painted metal storage unit from the 1940s next to a massive butcher block, or use a bleached pine table for a countertop. Don't hide dishes in cabinets; stack bowls on a baker's rack, slide plates vertically into an open holder on the wall, hook cups onto the pegs of a wooden hat rack. Overhead racks for hanging pans, utensils, and baskets also have become popular in country kitchens for their practicality and homey appeal.

**Hand-hewn wooden beams, ceramic floor tiles, brick walls, and a plaster ceiling all contribute to the rough-textured, rustic style of this kitchen.**
Design: Lillian Bogossian and Vivian Weil, Decorative Interiors; Photo: Steve Vierra

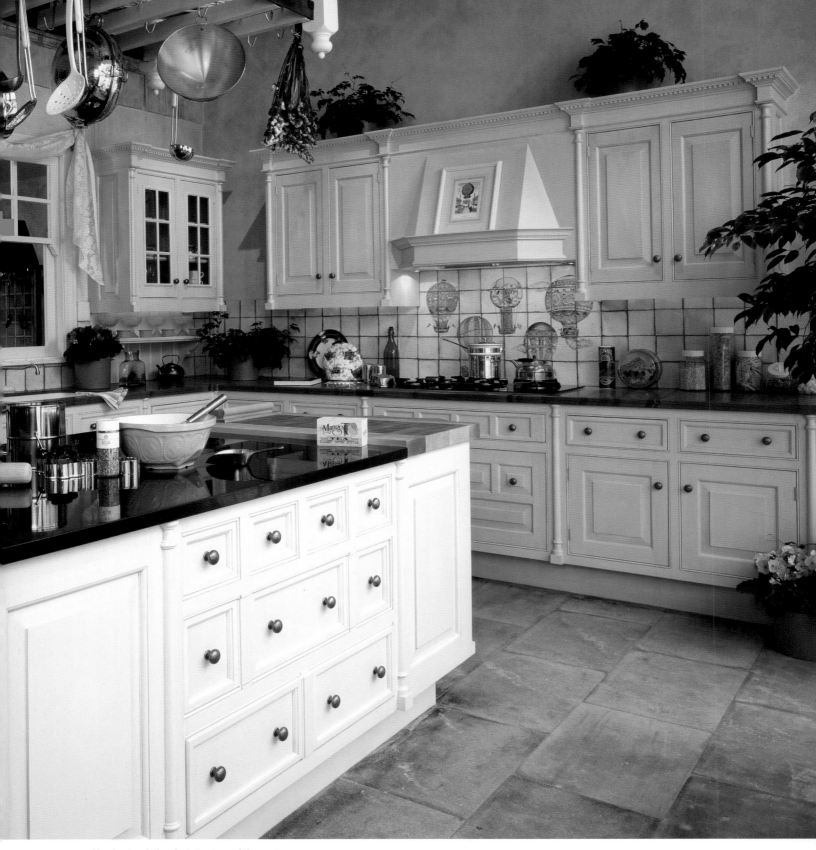

Hand-painted tiles depicting turn-of-the-century
hot-air balloons bring a fanciful touch to this
cottage kitchen. The workspace offers practical
features such as an overhead pot rack and a
built-in cutting board.

Photo courtesy of de Giulio kitchen design, inc.

Photo: Jeff Guerrant

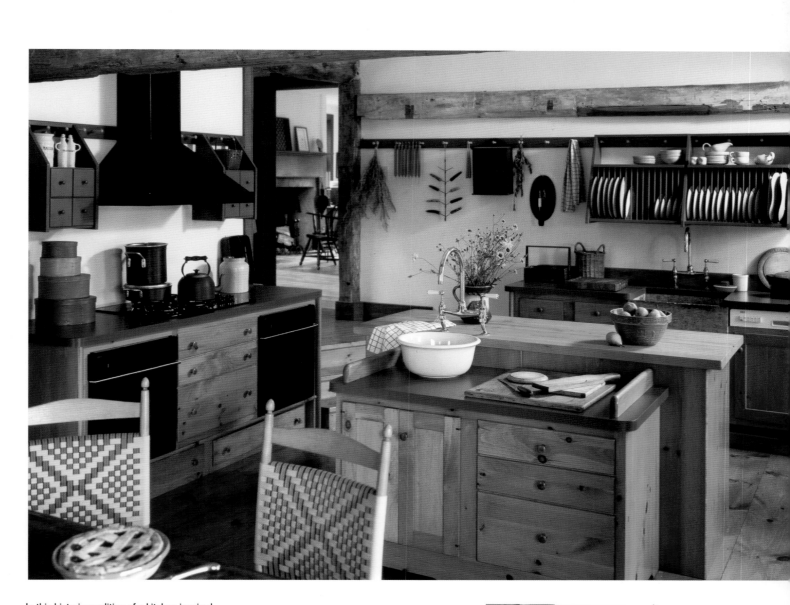

In this historic rendition of a kitchen inspired
by Shaker furniture, plate racks, spice drawers,
and dried herbs hang from a pegged rail wrapped
around the room. A plumbed wash bowl is in
keeping with the look, and a stack of four Shaker
boxes near the stovetop continues the theme.
Photo courtesy of Wood-Mode

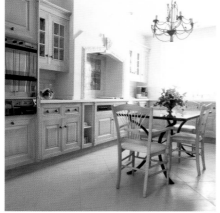

With its wheat-back chairs, plaster work, and
high ceilings, this kitchen has the feel of a
manor house in provincial France.
Photo courtesy of Paris Ceramics

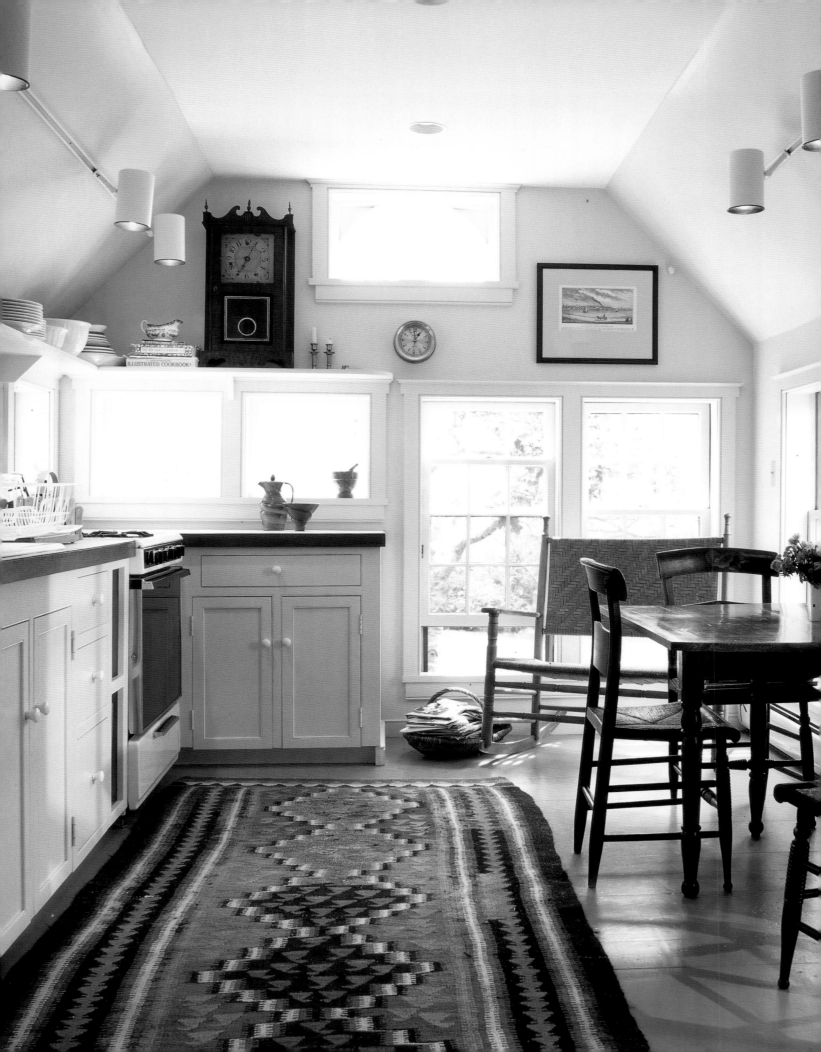

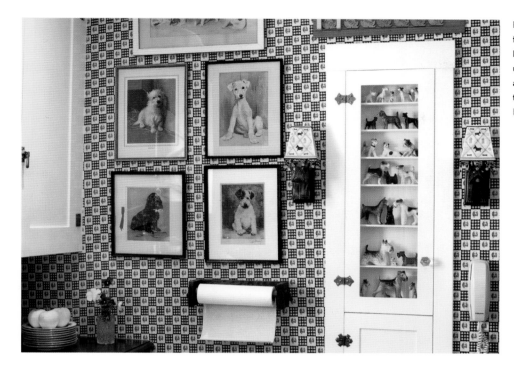

Everyone expects to see decorative accents focusing on fruit or vegetables in country kitchens, so a collection of canine prints and figurines is a surprising touch. Even though this is a small kitchen, the cohesiveness of the collection creates a distinctive personal identity.
Design: Elizabeth Klee Speert; Photos: Eric Roth

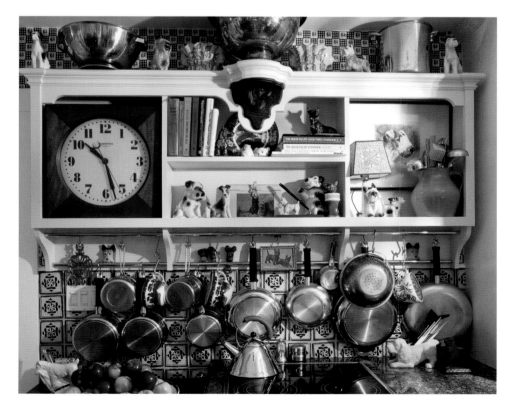

Opposite: A kitchen of limited dimensions needn't be claustrophobic. Here abundant windows, ivory-colored paint, open upper shelving, and a multi-layered lighting system contribute to an airy look. There's even room for a double rocking chair in the corner, a great vantage point for hungry friends during meal preparation. Photo: Eric Roth

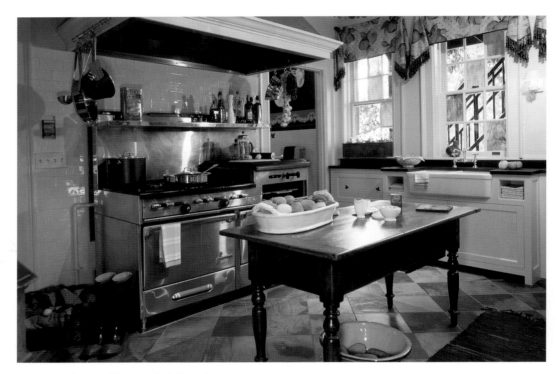

A simple farmhouse table is an affordable and flexible alternative to a built-in island.
Design: Benson Interiors; Photo: Peter Jaquith

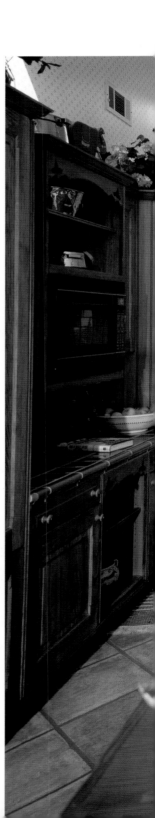

Traditional tiles, cheerful woven rugs, and paneled cabinetry featuring beaded insets contribute to the country ambience of this California kitchen. Above the windows, a display shelf extends between two glass-front cabinets, creating a clean line from soffit to soffit. Design: Neil Cooper, Cooper Pacific Kitchens; Photo: Tom Gordon; Photo courtesy of SieMatic

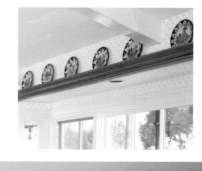

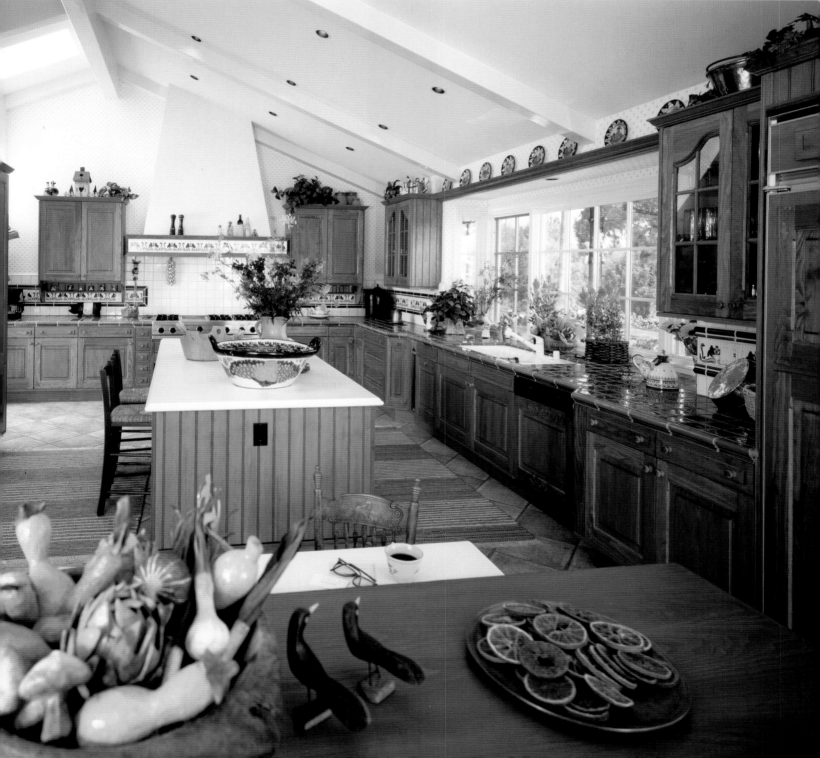

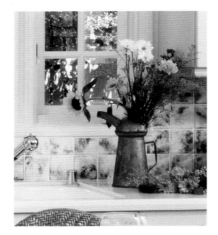

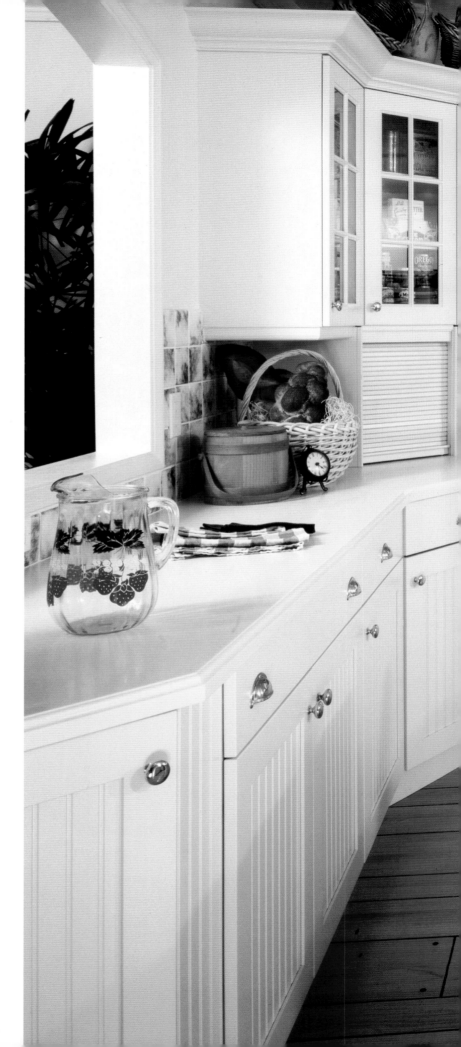

**White is a classic choice for cottage-style kitchens, as are cabinet doors with beaded insets and mullion glass.** Design: Julie Vagts, The Kitchen Works; Photo courtesy of Wood-Mode

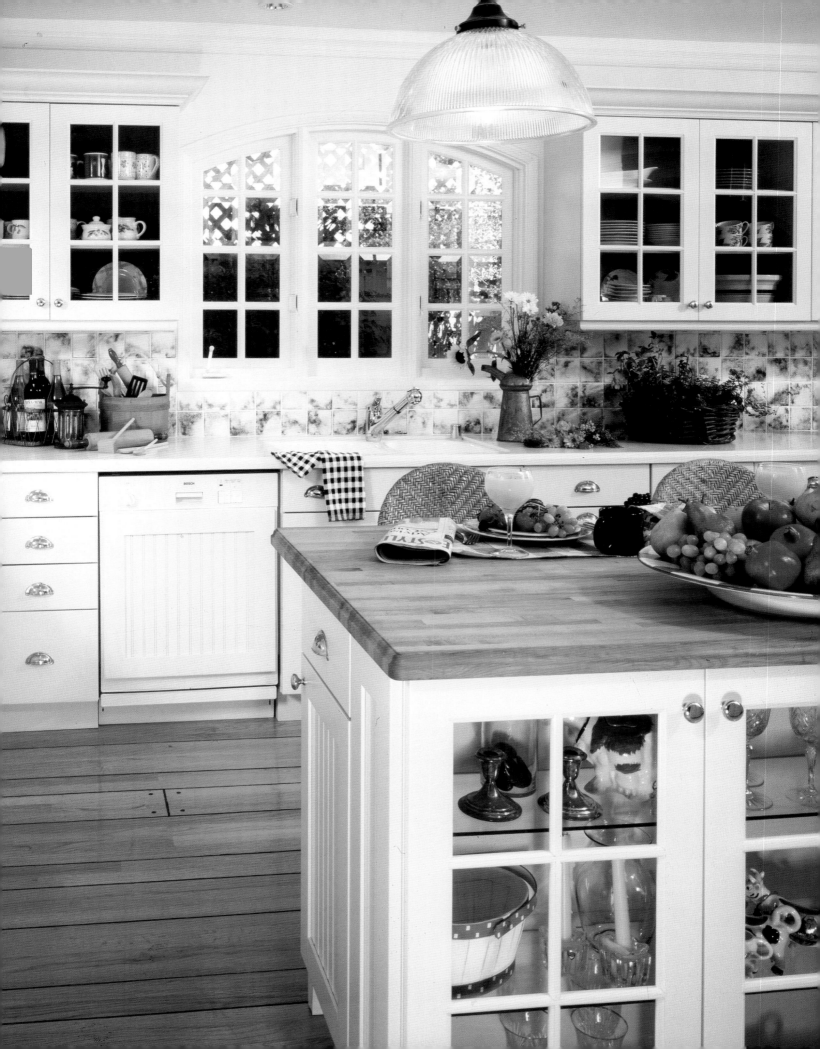

In this playful design, handcrafted cats and dogs
inhabit the room. Even the kitchen chairs, with
their wooden backs carved in the shape of fish,
carry out the whimsical theme.
Design: Stephen Huneck; Photo: Eric Roth

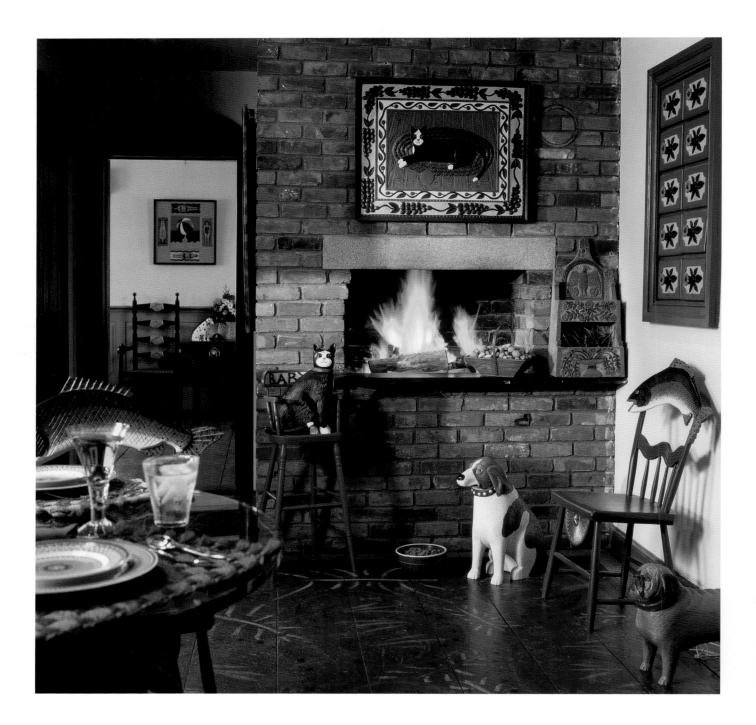

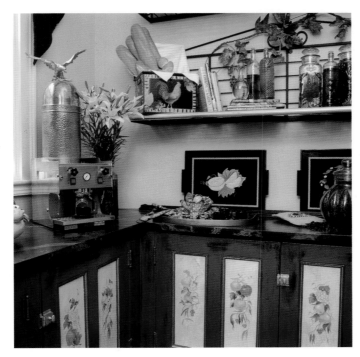

Special painting techniques transform wooden cupboard façades into works of art and prevent fitted cabinetry from becoming a visual liability. The charming botanicals on the cabinet fronts are bordered by weathered-looking surrounds, while the countertops are painted to look like green marble. Design: Jody Trail and Susan Maier, Trail-Maier Design; Photo: Steve Vierra

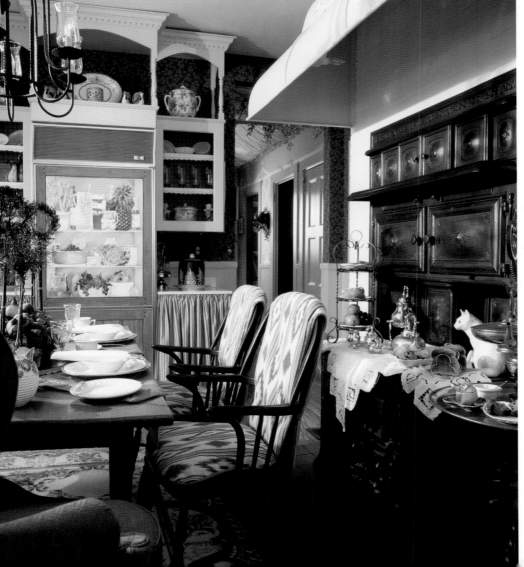

This eat-in kitchen offers a few surprises: a comfortable wing chair at the head of the breakfast table, a massive cast-iron stove serving as a sideboard, and a refrigerator with a trompe l'oeil façade showing shelves brimming with food. Design: Sandra J. Bissell Interior Design Photo: Eric Roth

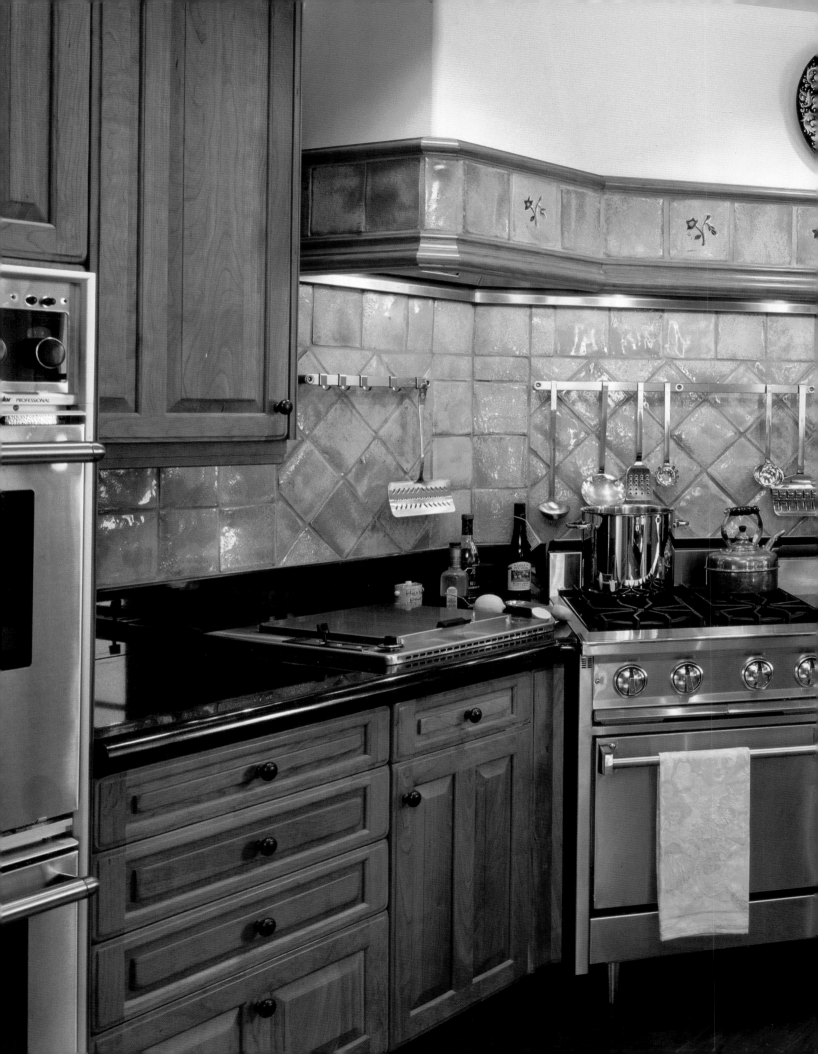

Previous pages: Utensil racks make finding
the right implement easy for cooks and can be
aesthetically striking. The forms of aluminum
spoons, spatulas, and other kitchen tools are
beautiful as they gleam in the light.
Design: Neil Cooper, Cooper Pacific Kitchens
Photo: Tom Gordon; Photo courtesy of SieMatic

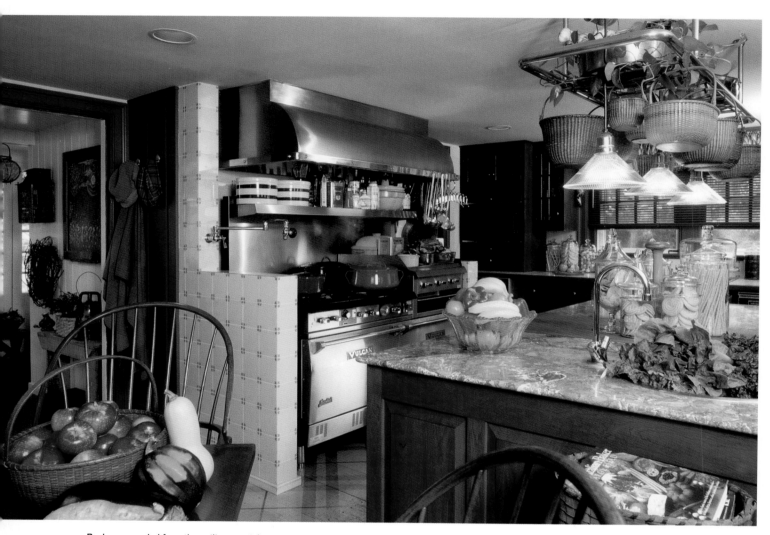

Racks suspended from the ceiling are right at
home in country-style kitchens, serving both
decorative and practical purposes. Showcase
a collection of baskets on a brass rack over a
center island. Design: Diane Chase Madden
Photo: Steve Vierra

To emphasize a collection, paint open shelves a
contrasting color. White pottery stands out against
a deep shade of paint. Design: Sue Adams
Interiors; Photo: Peter Jaquith

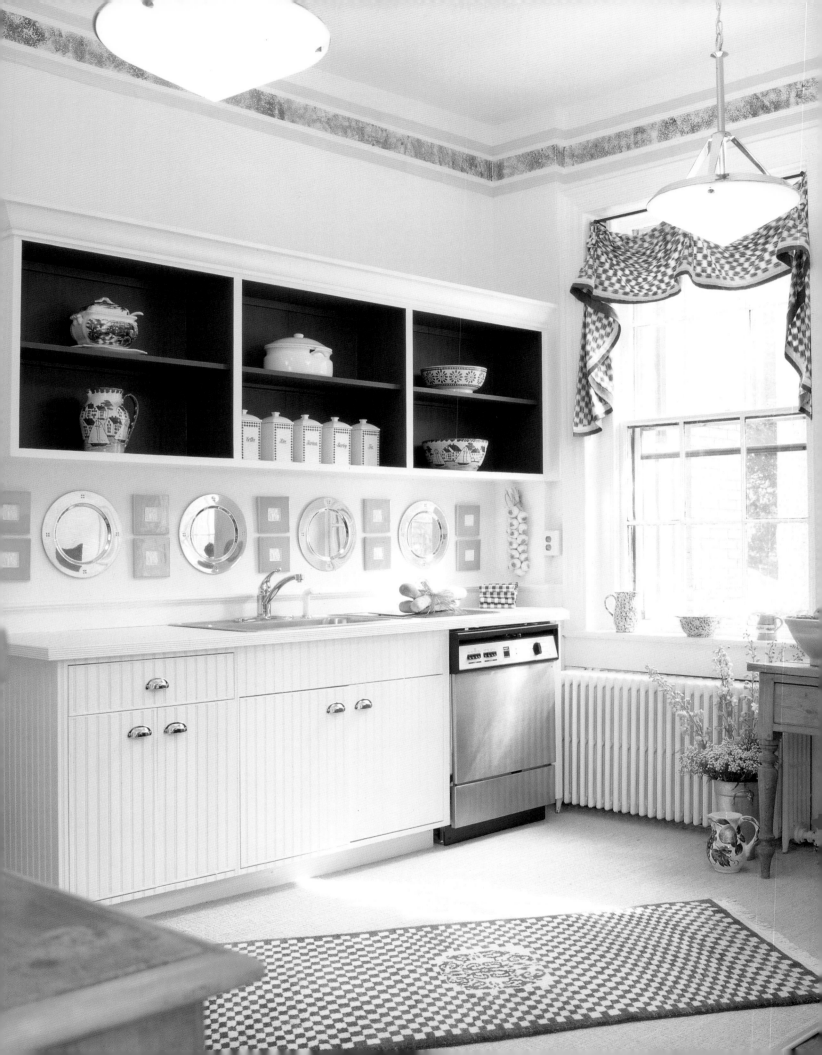

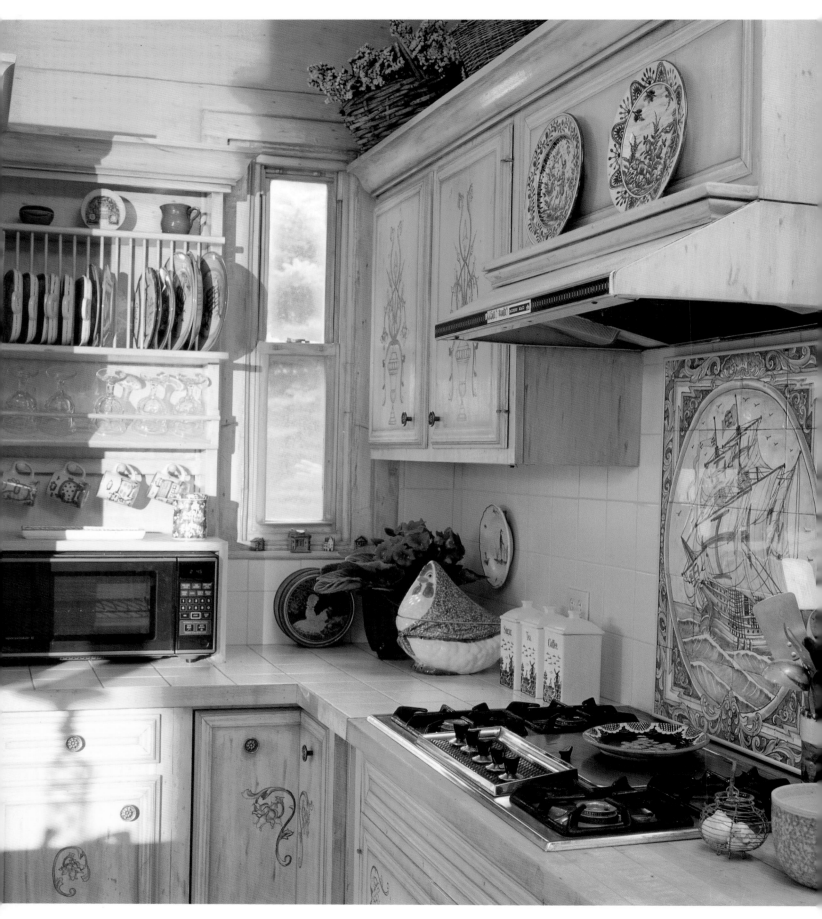

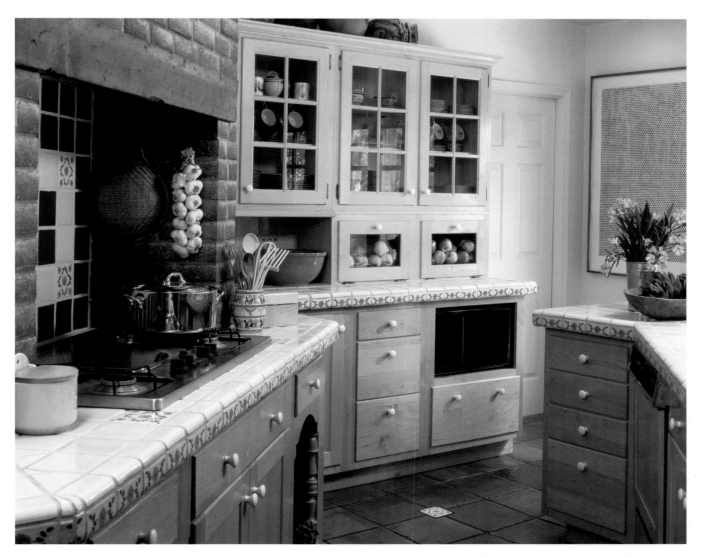

Terra-cotta and glazed decorative tiles, arched cabinet openings with turned posts, and a collection of clay pottery convey a country style rooted in the Southwest.
Photo courtesy of Wood-Mode

Stenciling adds a decorative element to natural pine cabinets, whose pale façades keep the space from becoming dark. Dishware visible in the open plate rack and on hooks adds to the casual look. Behind the cooktop, blue tiles depicting a sailing ship add another charming dimension. Design: Faye Etter Interior Design
Photo: Eric Roth

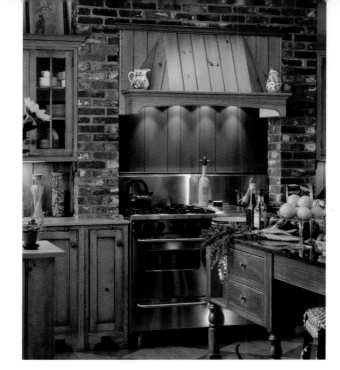

In this visually warm kitchen, a stained checker-board pattern enlivens the floor and complements the pine cabinetry's rich patina. A custom-designed stained table serves as an island, yet has the country flair of freestanding furniture.
Design: Phyllis D. Greene Interiors
Photos: Peter Jaquith

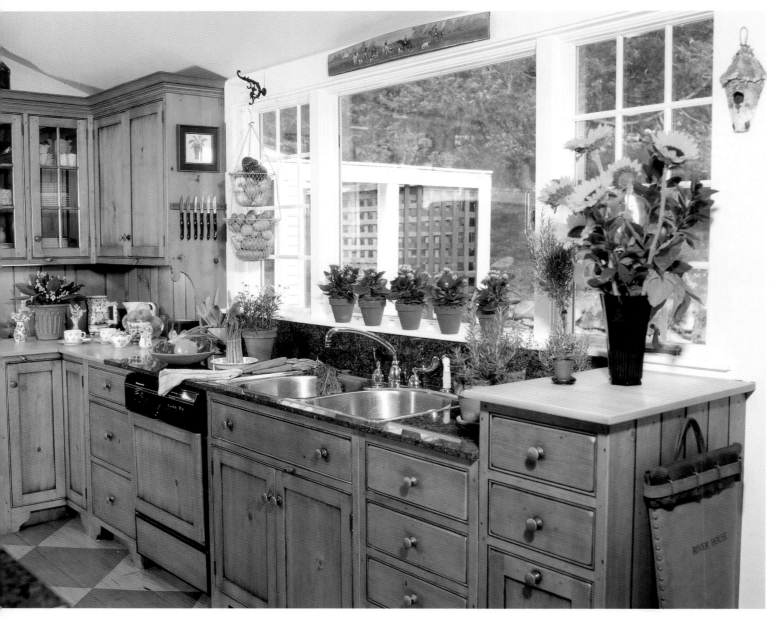

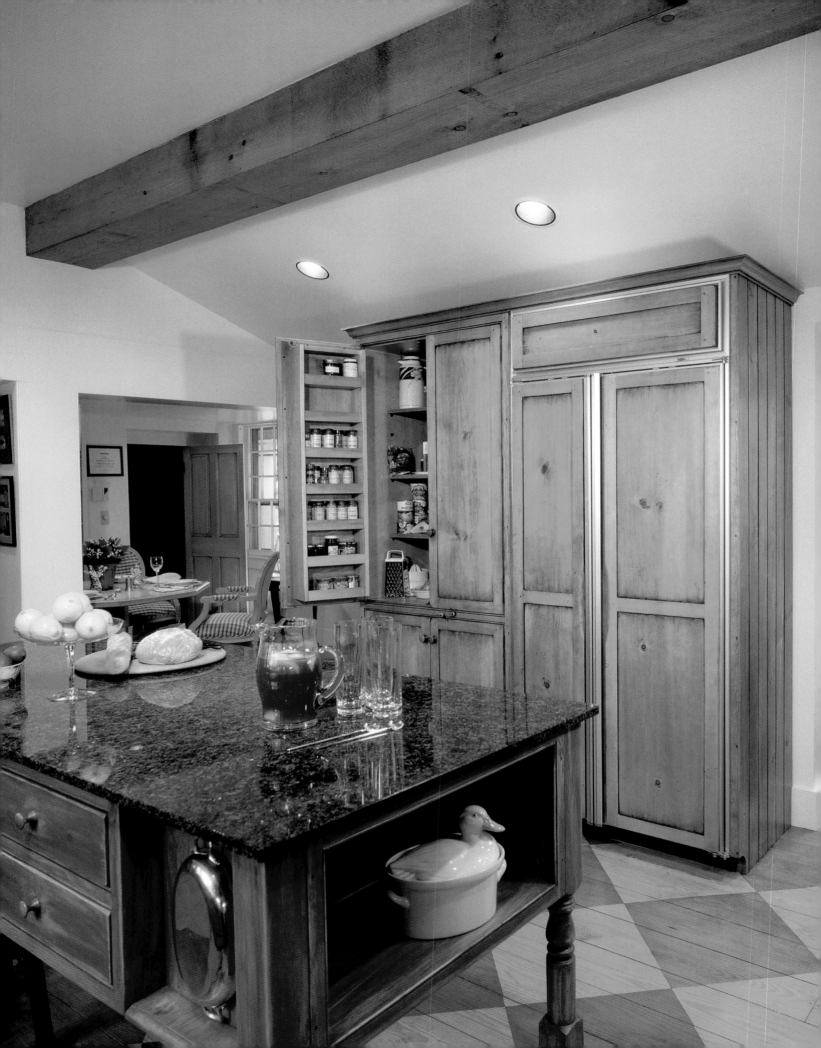

Many country designs build on the natural affi█
between the garden and kitchen. In this simple█
appealing room, pots of herbs in a sunny wind█
underscore the connection between cultivation█
and cooking. A wreath of red chilies and braids█
garlic and peppers continue the motif of garde█
freshness. Design: Diane Hughes Interiors
Photos: Steve Vierra

Getting things out in the open is a popular strategy
in country kitchen design. Pots and pans, cooking
staples, crockery, collectibles, and utensils create
a look of ordered, hightly functional abundance.
Design: Carole Harmon, White House Farm
Photo: Eric Roth

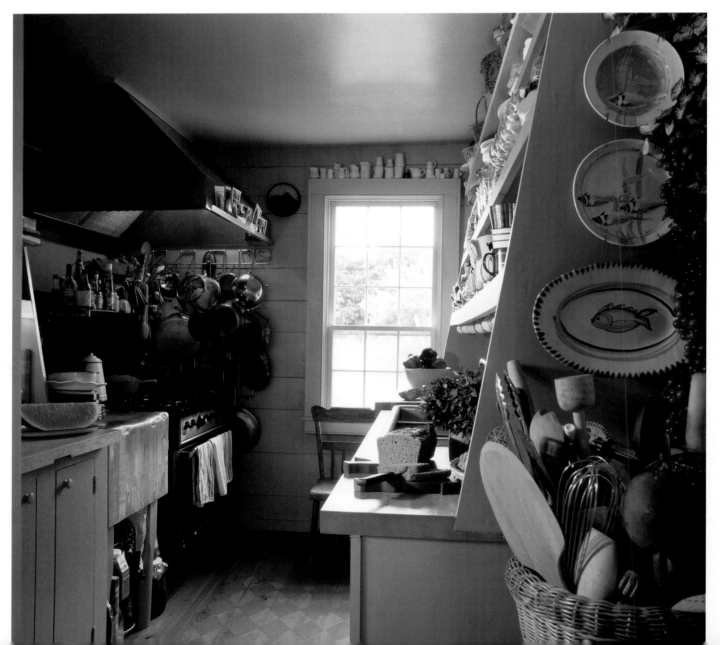

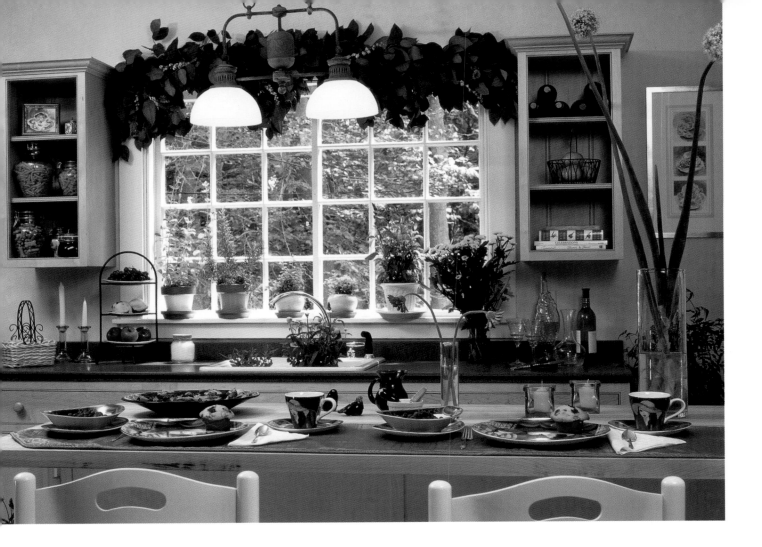

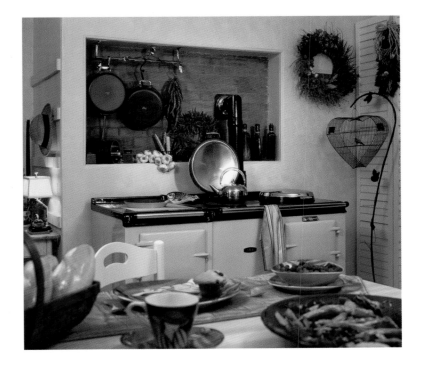

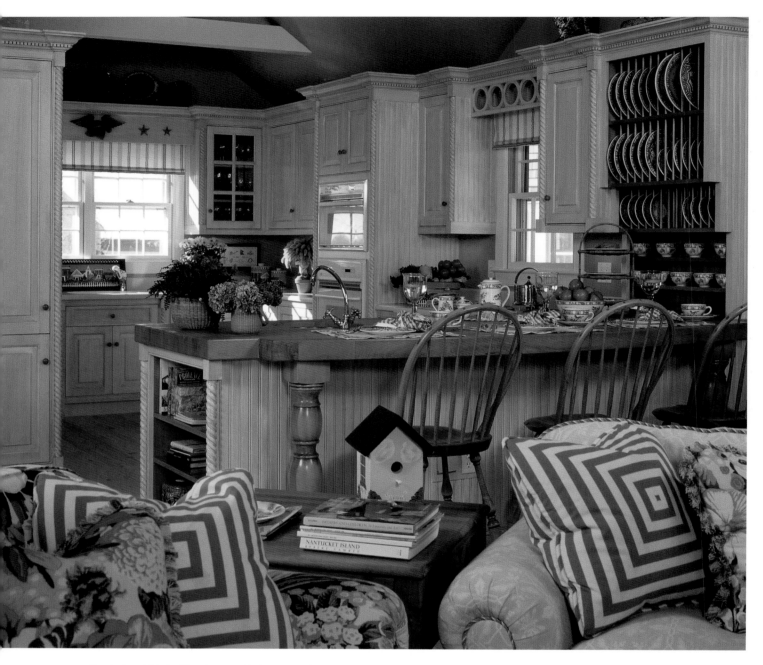

The design of this traditional country kitchen invites interaction by offering seating on Windsor-style chairs at the bar area and on overstuffed sofas in the nearby family room. A blue-and-white palette is carried through both rooms, visually uniting them. Design: Anthony Catalfano Interiors Photo: Steve Vierra

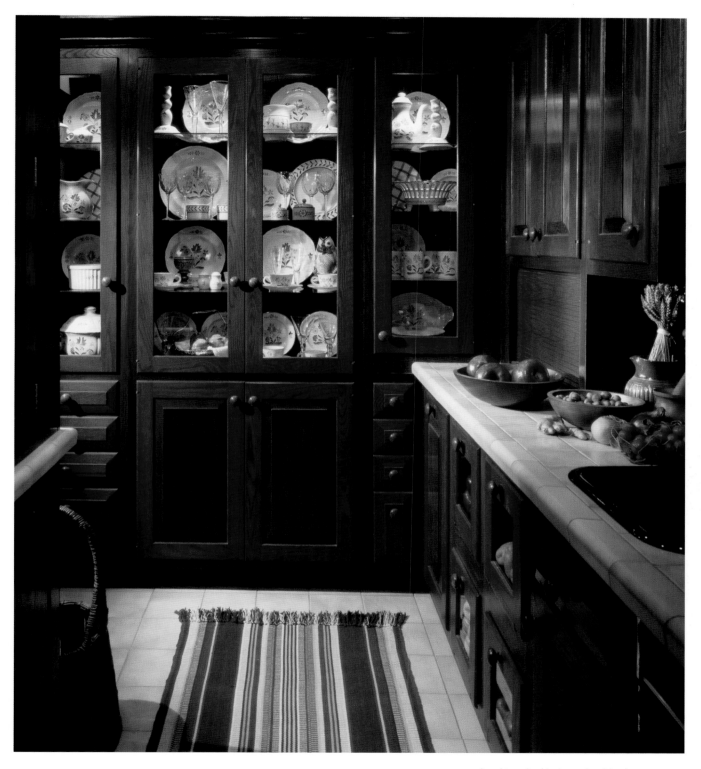

Jewel-toned cabinetry and a striped woven rug
give this butler's pantry an unusual Nordic flavor.
Photo courtesy of Wood-Mode

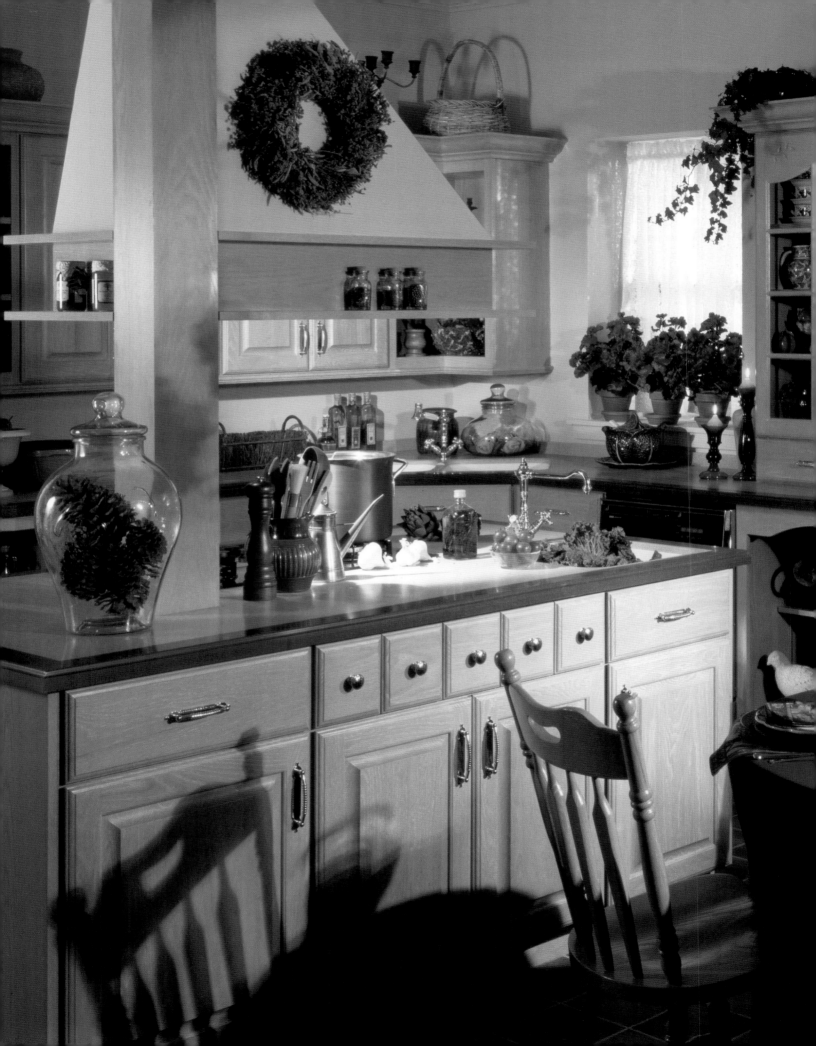

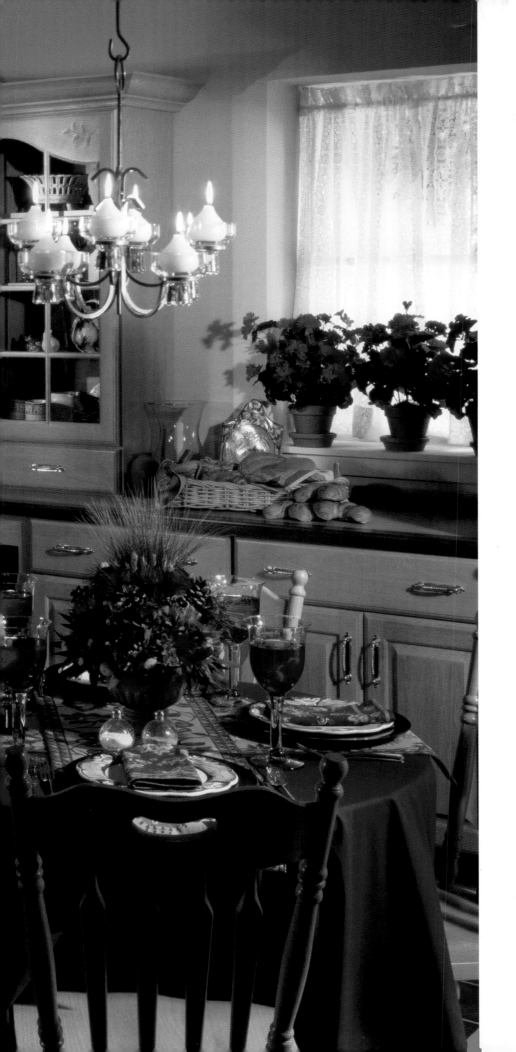

Light-colored kitchens strike a cheerful note. As an alternative to white-painted cabinets, finish wood with a white glaze to let the character of the wood grain show through.
Photo courtesy of Wood-Mode

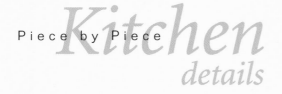

Piece by Piece Kitchen *details*

*Thanks to the vast range of details available from craftspeople and manufacturers, planning country kitchens is a joy for homeowners. Choose from idiosyncratic tiles, farmhouse sinks, European-style cabinetry, and old-time drawer pulls.*

*Storage Options*

Options for storing kitchen items in the open abound in country interiors, from built-in plate racks and glass-front cabinetry to freestanding work islands with open racks and shelving (below).

Center photo design: Phyllis D. Greene Interiors

Photo: Peter Jaquith

Bottom photo courtesy of Crate and Barrel

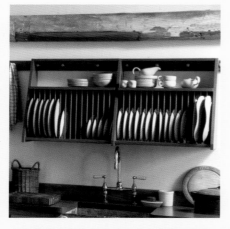

*Ceramic Accents*

Ceramic tiles, with handcrafted styling and easy-to-clean surfaces, accent kitchen work areas—countertops, sinks, stoves (below).

Top photo courtesy of Waterworks

Bottom photo courtesy of Paris Ceramics

*Water Ways*

Sinks inspired by old-time kitchens or decorated with natural motifs work well in country interiors (below).

Photos courtesy of Kohler

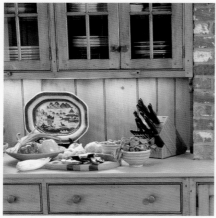

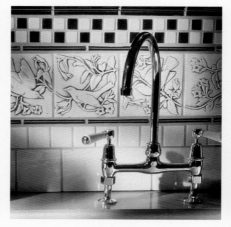

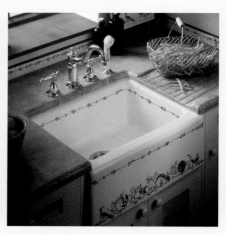

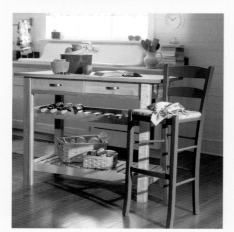

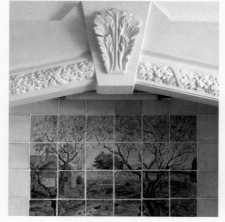

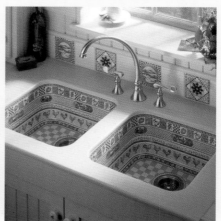

*Counter Effects*

Countertops that give the country look range
from wood or tile to a new country alternative,
polished granite. Stone counters can be an
effective foil for wood cabinets (below).

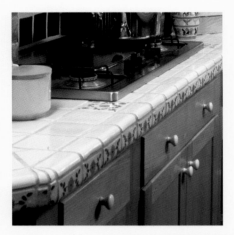

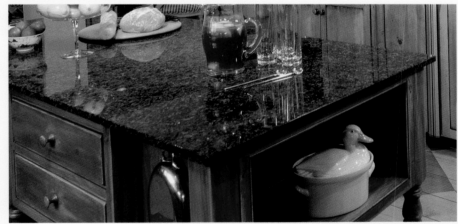

*Country Hardware*

Look for metal, porcelain, and wood drawer pulls
and knobs, small but important kitchen details,
to convey a country style (below).

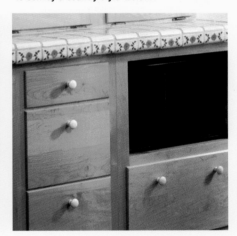

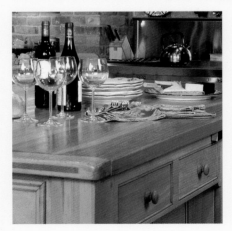

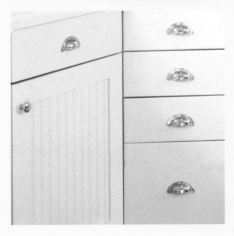

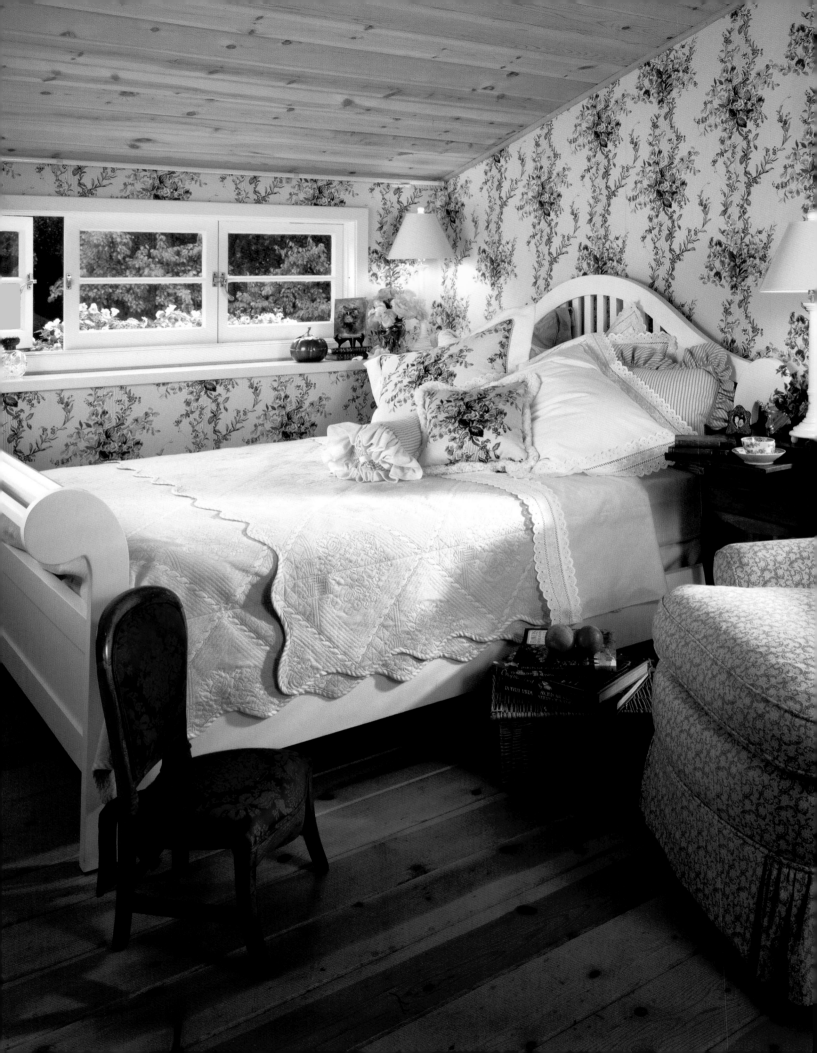

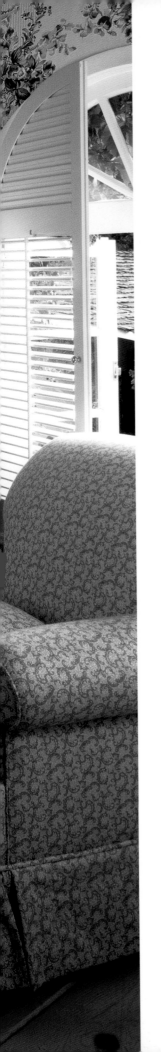

# *Country* Bedrooms

*Drifting into sleep and waking in the country is a delicious experience. On a summer night, a horse neighs in the distance; breezes carry the scent of an apple orchard through open windows. At dawn, moonlight and shadows give way to an ethereal rosy tint. A timeless, comforting quality—as well as a perennial freshness—infuses the rhythms of daybreak and nightfall.*

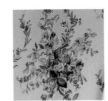

Those same qualities—timeless and comforting, yet with fresh appeal—apply to well-designed country-style bedrooms, whether in a truly pastoral setting or amid an unsleeping cityscape. To achieve timelessness, incorporate antiques and reproductions, such as painted blanket chests, marble-topped washstands, and rough-hewn cupboards. Canopy and four-poster bedsteads, still extremely popular centuries after being introduced, always can be counted on to create a classic country ambience. But also look for opportunities for freshness and surprise—a headboard made to look like a cottage fence, a weathered window frame transformed into a mirror, pillows in the most outrageous colors of a crazy quilt spread across the bed.

Comfort and warmth, important elements of all country interiors, are absolutely essential to bedrooms. Textiles make a vital contribution here, with bed linens and down comforters turning the bed itself into an irresistible nest.

Rugs—from colonial-style braided ovals to contemporary Scandinavian weavings—protect bare feet from cold floors.

Numerous other practical considerations come into play in bedroom design. Ample dimmable light—whether converted brass kerosene lamps or, for new country style, halogen lamps in the modern idiom—flexes for reading, conversation, or romance. Storage is another concern, as bedrooms typically double as dressing rooms. Hatboxes and steamer trunks are longtime favorites for country bedrooms; picnic baskets with lids and stacked vintage suitcases are among the less conventional possibilities.

Aside from practical matters, remember that the bedroom is where we experience the most vulnerable moments of life: crossing the line between sleep and consciousness, sharing intimate moments, and recharging in quiet solitude. Choose colors, fabrics, and furnishings that not only express your personality but also blend harmoniously to create a tranquil, country-style retreat.

Varnished pine floors, a country staple, are complemented by a ceiling of natural pine that is light enough to reflect rather than absorb illumination. The white lamps, bed, woodwork, and shutters also help keep the room from seeming closed in.
Photo: Furniture and fabrics by Summer Hill Ltd.

123

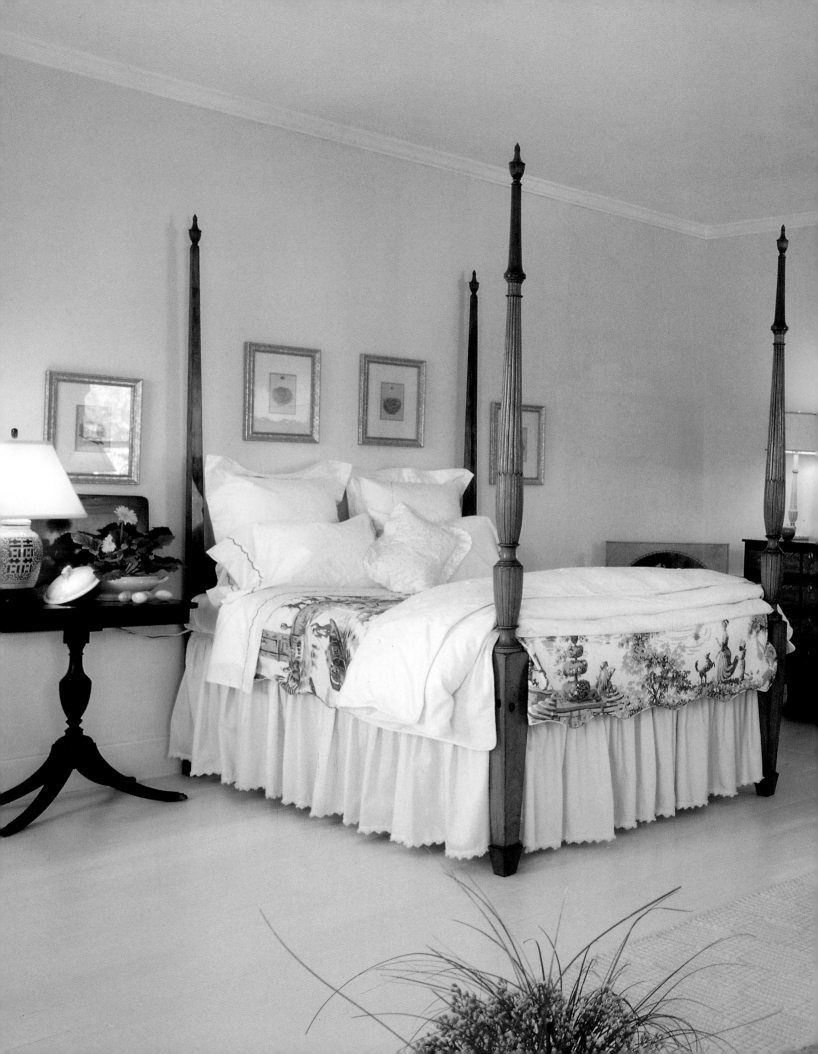

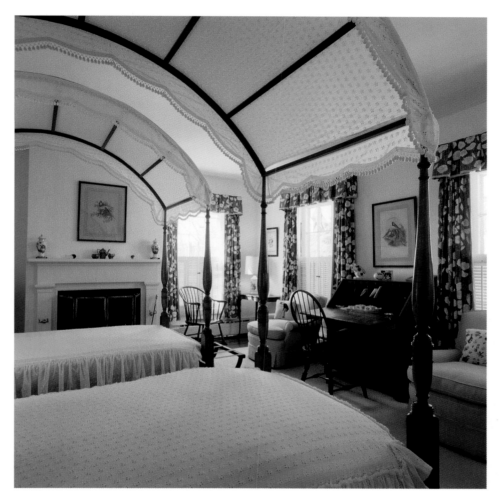

Twin beds sometimes seem like poor cousins to their full-size counterparts, but canopies elevate them to grander status in this comfortable room. Design: Austin Patterson Disston Architects; Photo: Fred George

Painting floors with smooth ivory enamel brightens bedrooms for a cheerful look. Potted plants are a nice touch in the boudoir as well as in other rooms of the house. Design: Kay Bailey McKallagat Design and Decoration Photo: Peter Jaquith

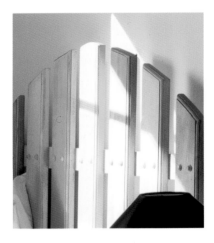

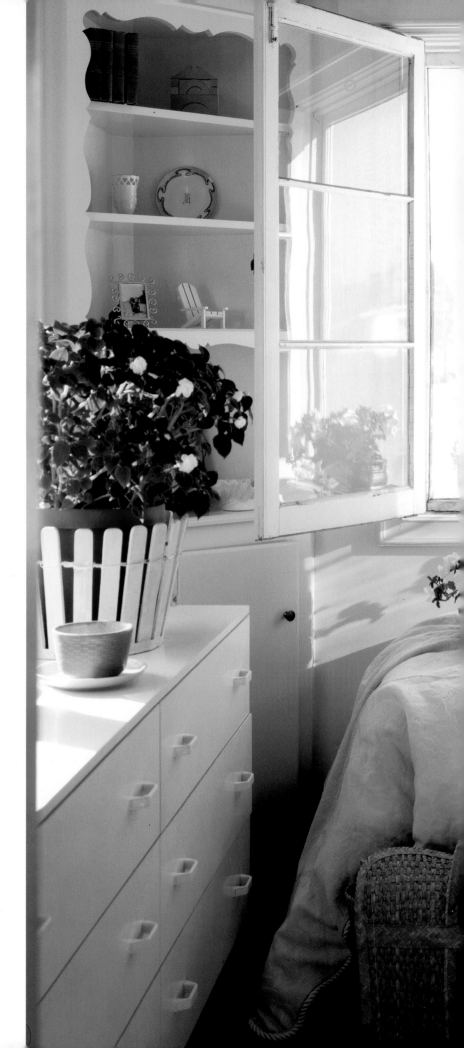

Cottage style can be achieved with little effort and minimal expense because the desired look is unaffected. Furniture in this room doesn't match in a traditional sense, but continuity arises from the scale and down-to-earth attitude of the clean-lined contemporary bureau, natural wood bedside table, and headboard inspired by outdoor fencing. Design: Joe Ruggiero
Photo: Tim Street-Porter

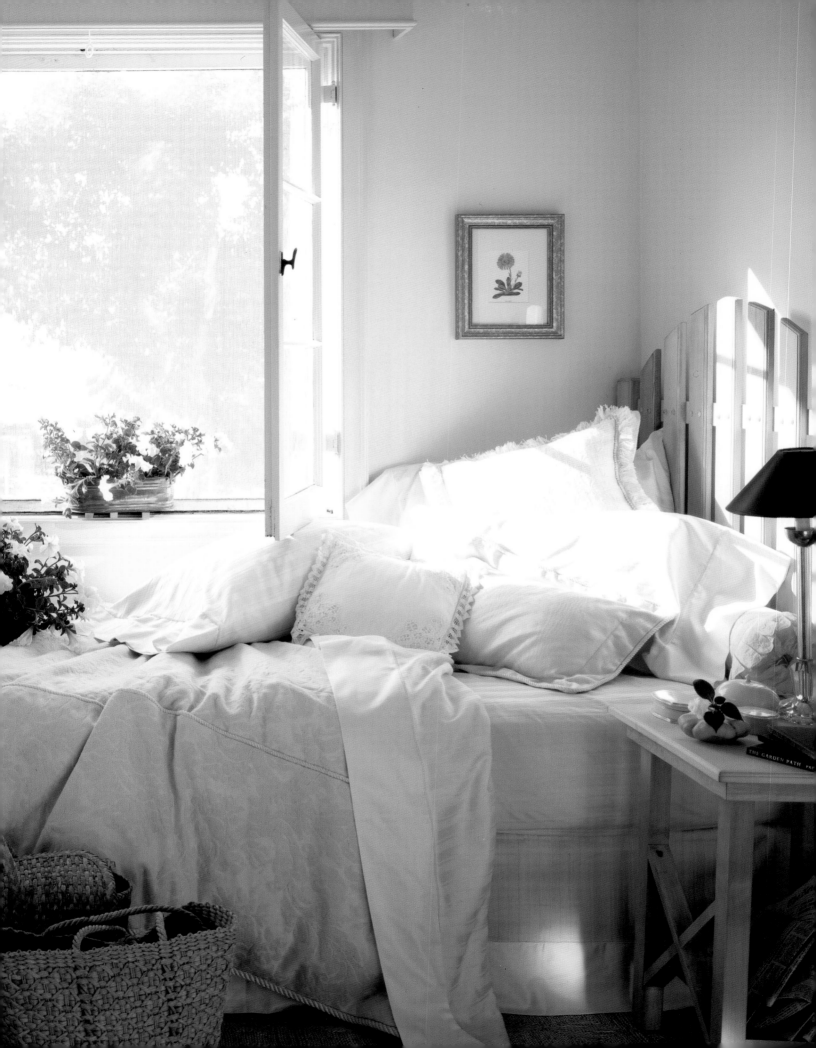

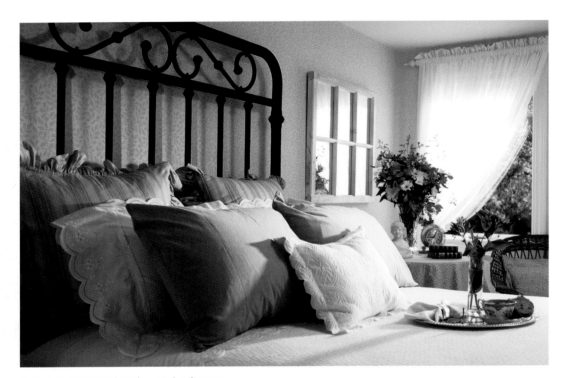

Hang a mirror mounted inside a window frame to give the illusion of space and to add brightness by reflecting available light. A pale neutral palette, wicker furniture, and sheer white window treatment also contribute to the luminous, airy ambience. Design: Susan Allen
Photo: Steve Vierra

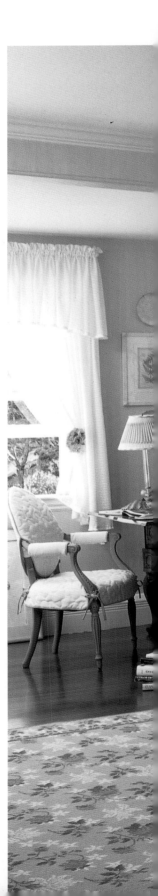

Out-of-the-ordinary hues, such as the green of young woodland ferns in spring, create refreshing pastoral bedrooms. Design: Gary McBournie
Photo: Steve Vierra

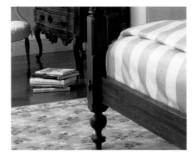

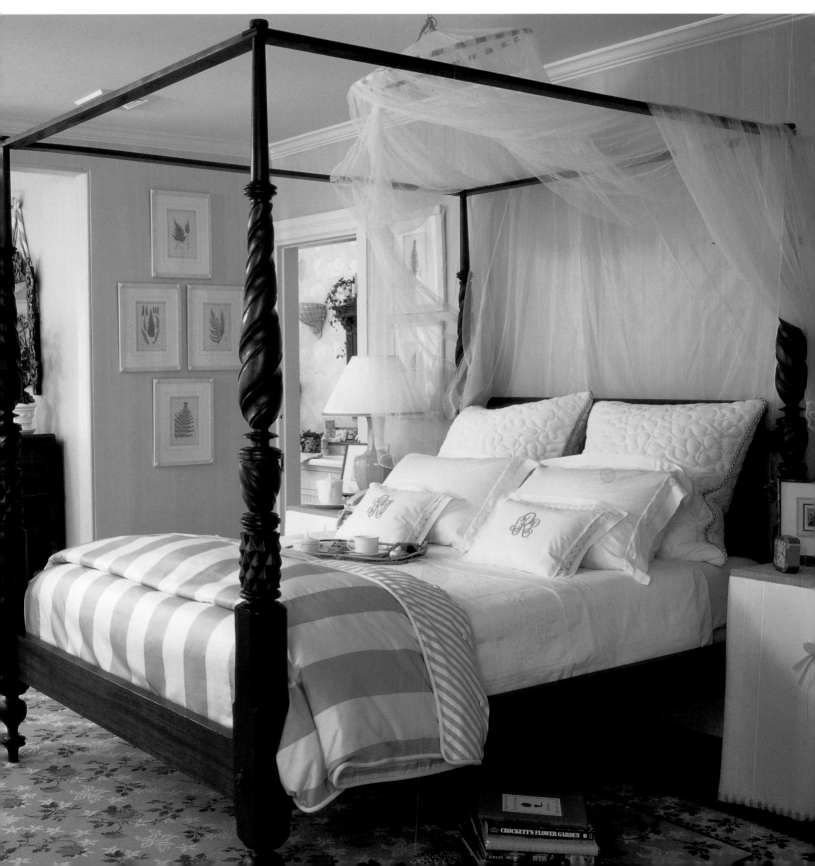

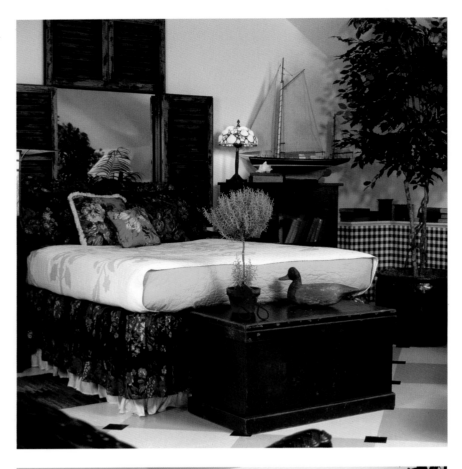

A narrow shelf running around a room like wainscoting helps organize model ships, photographs, and books that might otherwise become too cluttered. A mirrored headboard incorporates weathered shutters in an unusual design. Design: Judy Collins and Bob Collins, Peach Tree Designs; Photos: Steve Vierra

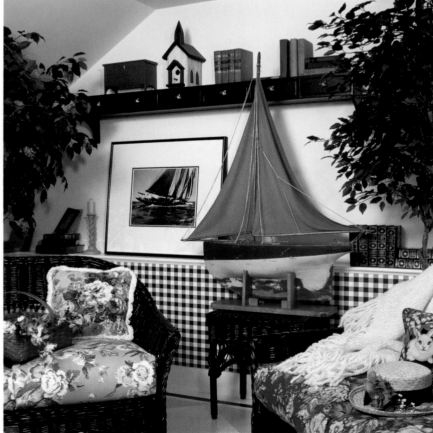

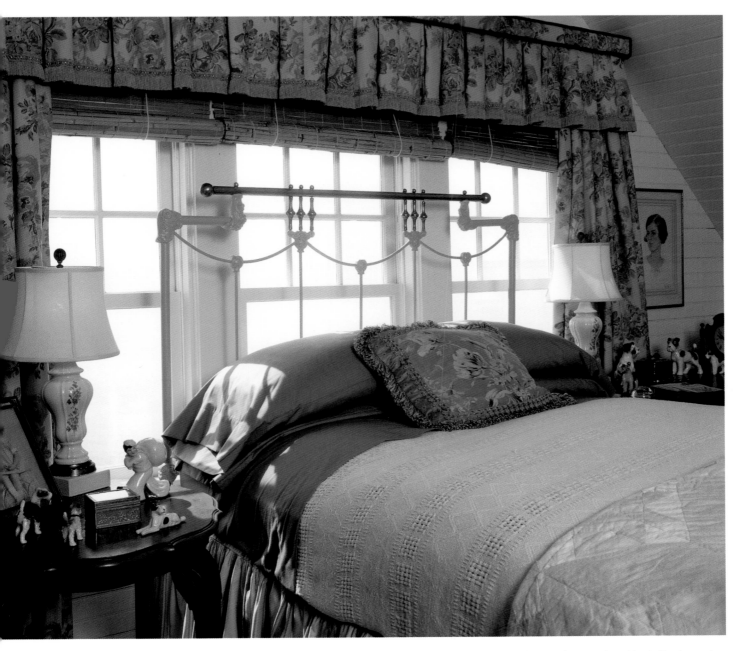

Design an unassuming yet thoroughly inviting bedroom with old-time ambience using a blend of basic country elements: an old family quilt, an antique brass-and-iron bedstead, bead-board wall and ceiling paneling, and a blend of floral and striped fabrics with a tea-stained look. Design: Elizabeth Klee Speert; Photo: Steve Vierra

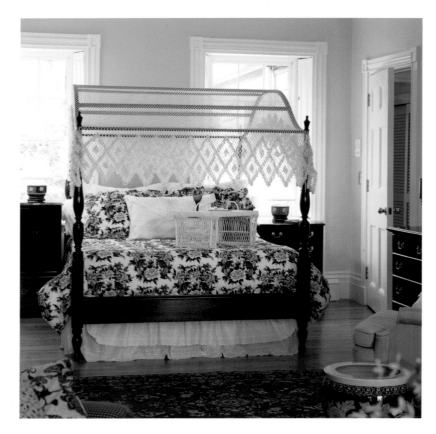

A crocheted canopy creates a sense of protection without becoming claustrophobic or obscuring views. Design: Constance Gallagher Interior Design; Photo: Peter Jaquith

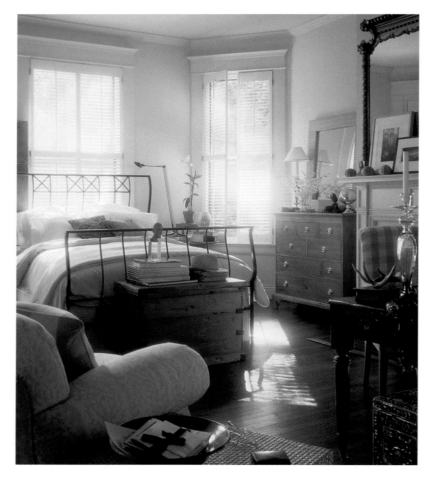

A beige palette is anything but boring in this sun-splashed bedroom. The scrubbed pine surface of a chest of drawers and a trunk contrast with the shiny brass drawer pulls, iron bed frame, and understated fabrics for a warm, restful retreat. Photo: Kenton Robertson, courtesy of Milling Road

A play of contrasts fuels this room's appeal, from the light color and sleek texture of the furniture to the dark, rough-hewn walls and beams. Photo courtesy of Weatherend Estate Furniture

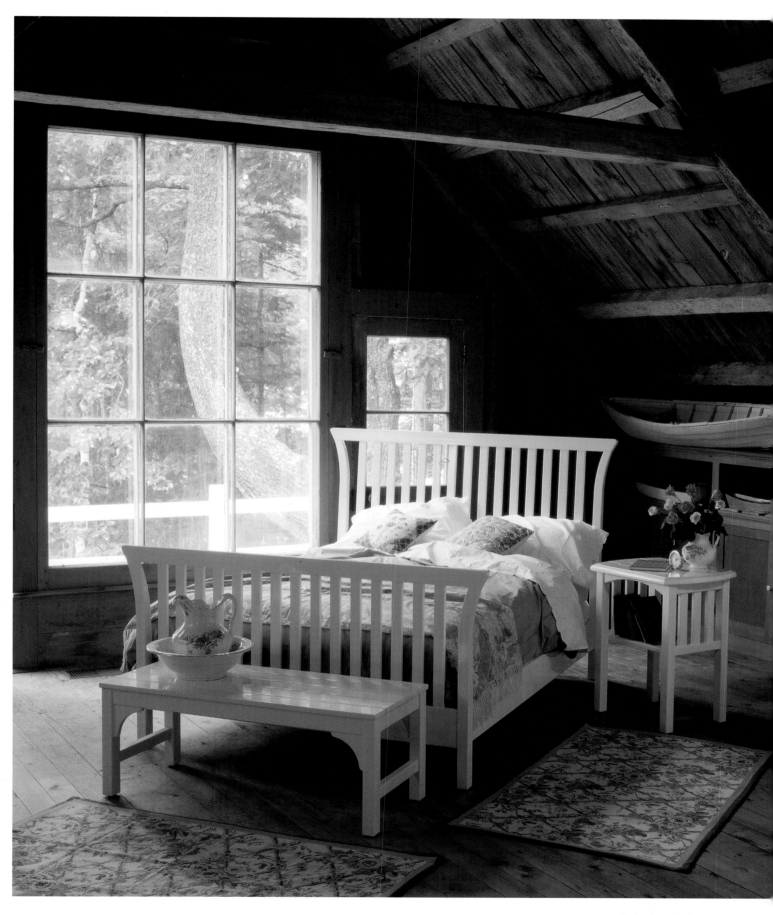

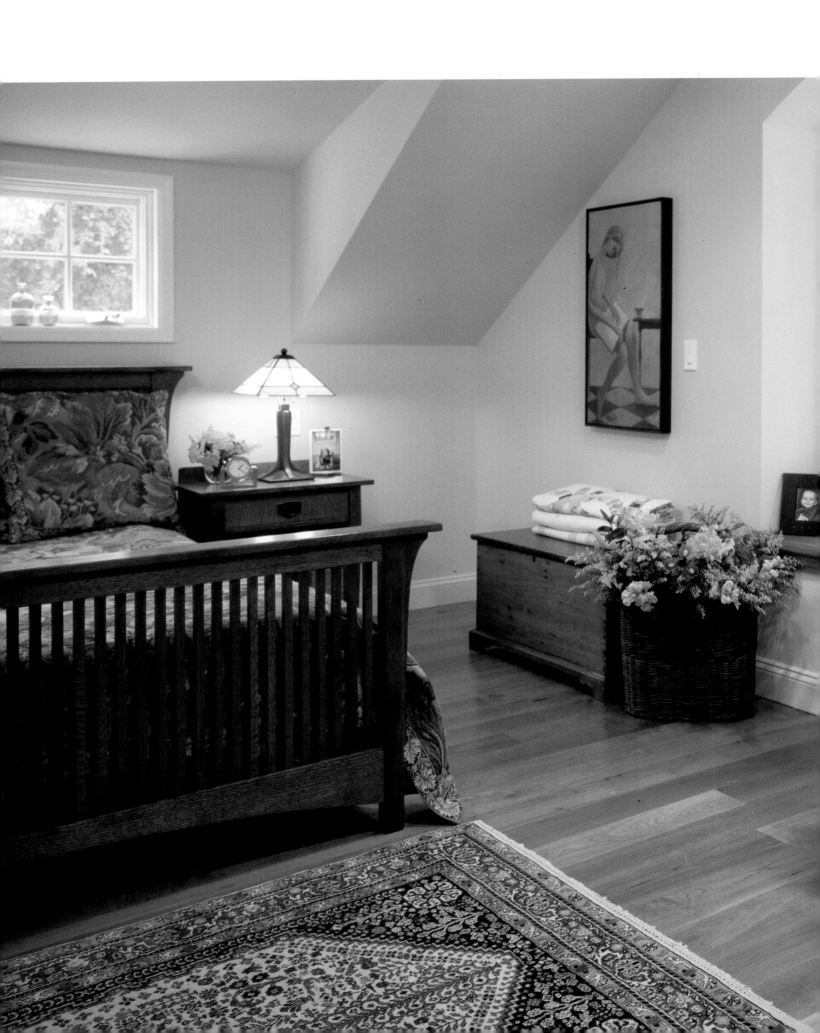

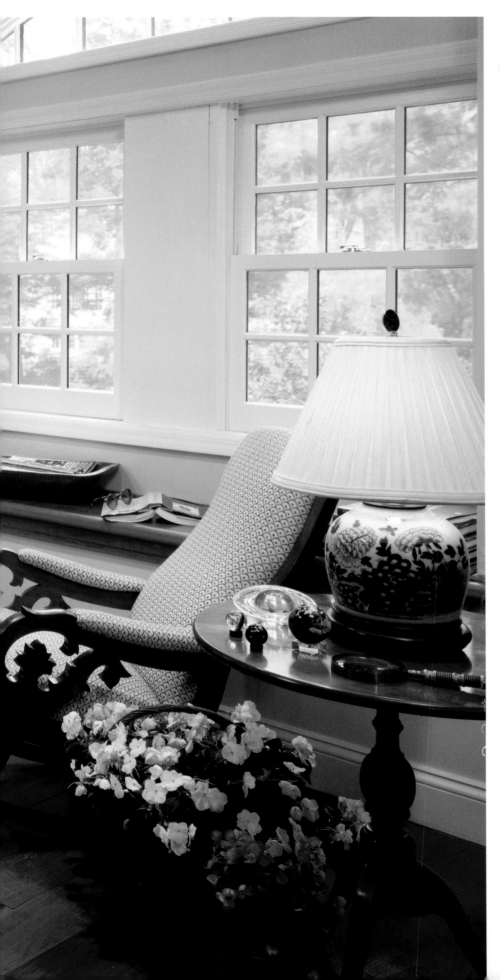

The grained oak and sturdy styling of the Arts and Crafts movement, seen here in the bed and bedside table, contribute to a down-to-earth look that is ideal for country interiors and easily blends with furniture from various periods.
Design: Gustavson/Dundes; Photo: Peter Paige

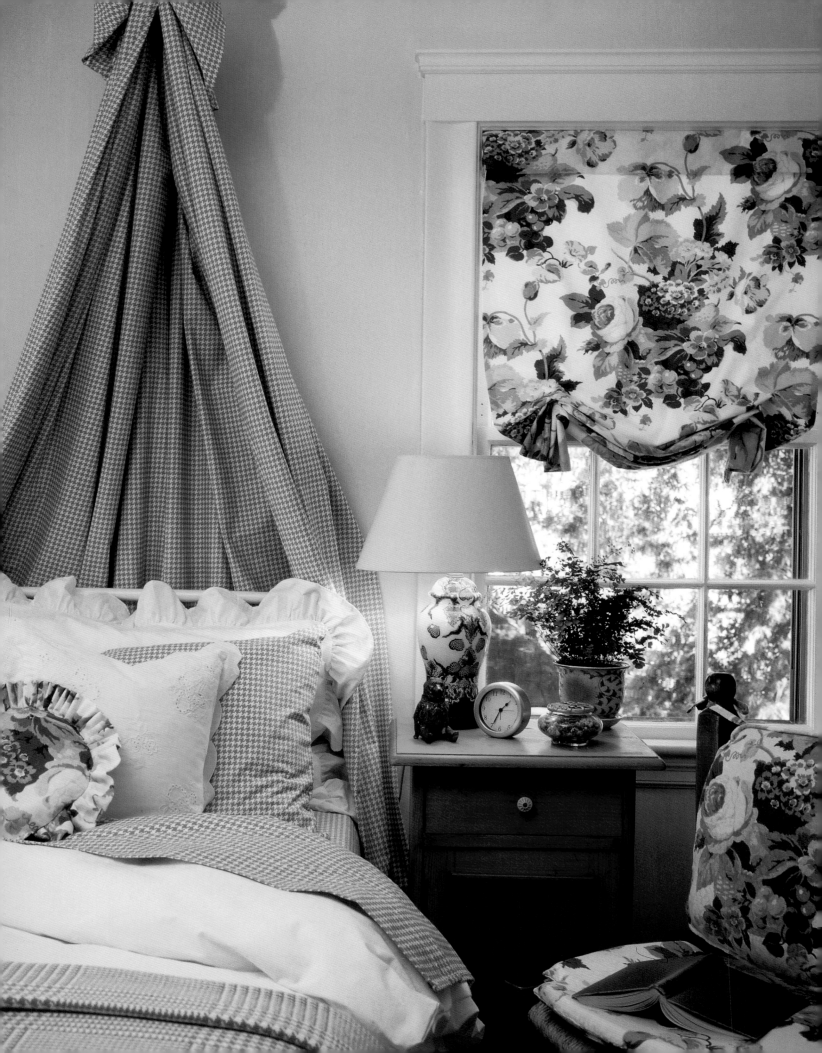

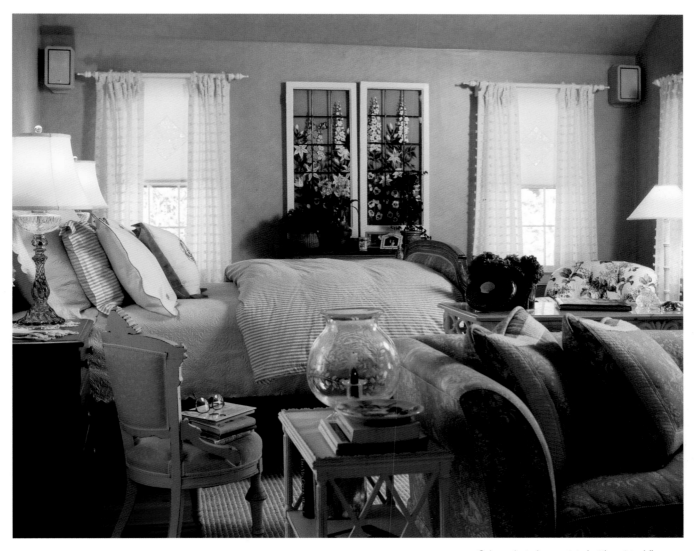

Salvaged windows painted with a virtual flower garden reinforce this lovely room's springlike colors and patterns. Design: Anthony Catalfano Interiors; Photo: Steve Vierra

Draped fabric, gathered at the ceiling and fanned around a headboard, inexpensively creates the look of a canopy bed. Design: Eleanor E. Samuels, Abbott Interiors; Photo: Peter Jaquith

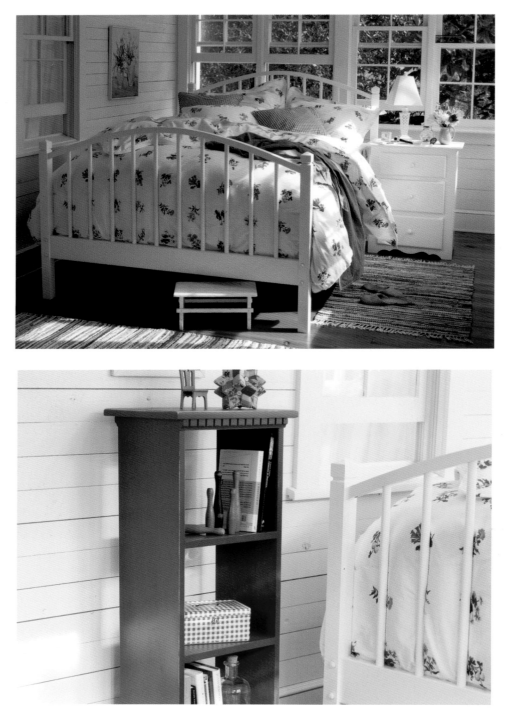

Colorful rag rugs enliven cottage bedrooms and
inspire fabrics and accessories that pick up on
reds, yellows, and blues. Against a white back-
ground, primary colors strike a cheerful chord.
Photos courtesy of Crate and Barrel

A checked floor, striped woven rug, plaid pillows
and floral and gingham fabrics come together in
this sunny, cozy New England bedroom. A primitive
portrait in the style of early American itinerant
artists fits in with the room's period look.
Design: Lillian August; Photo: Bill Rothschild

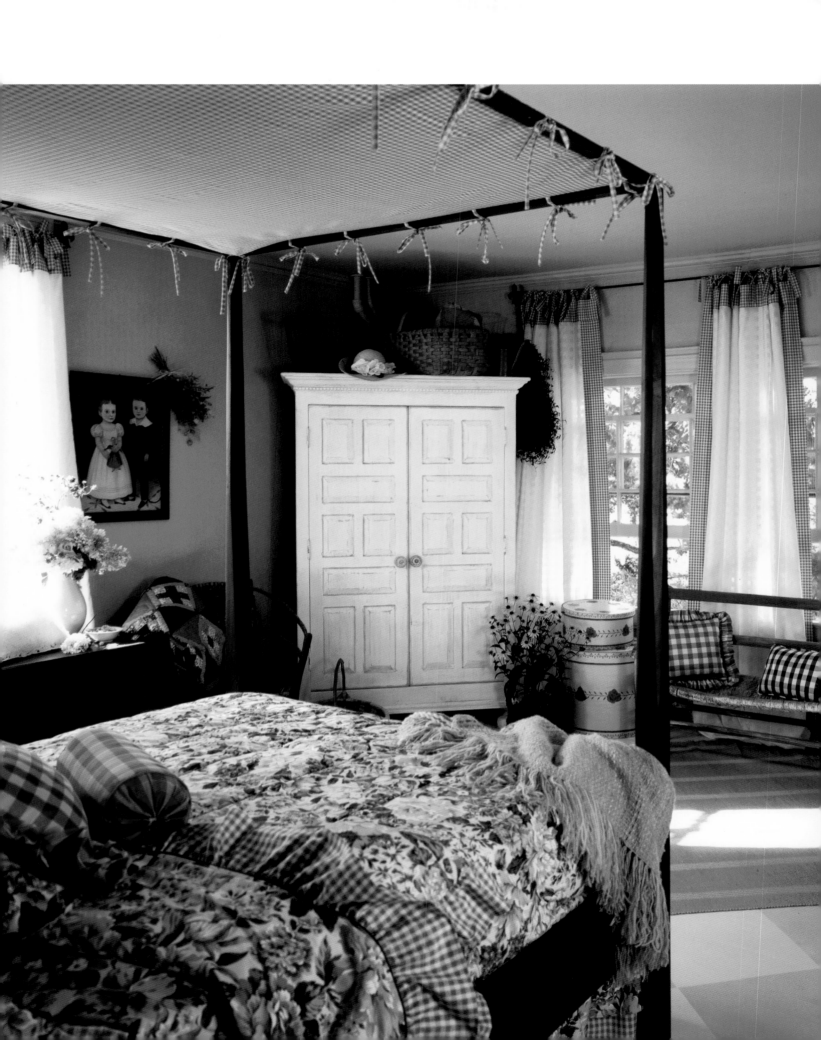

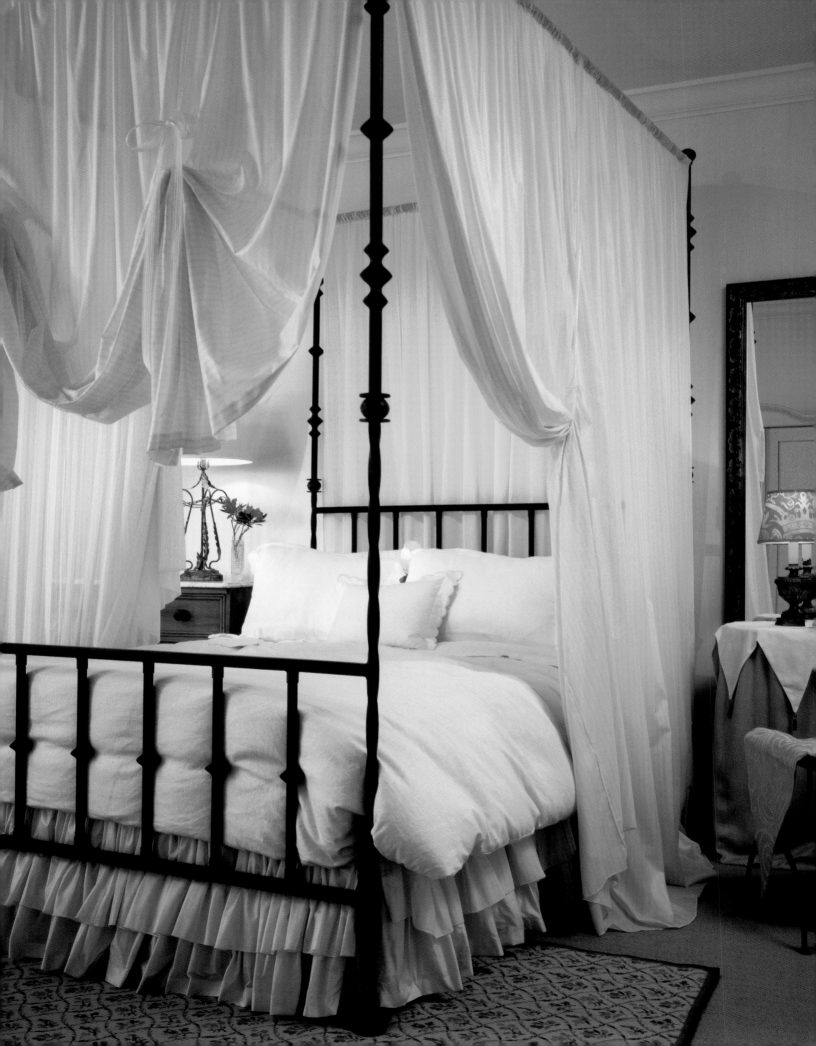

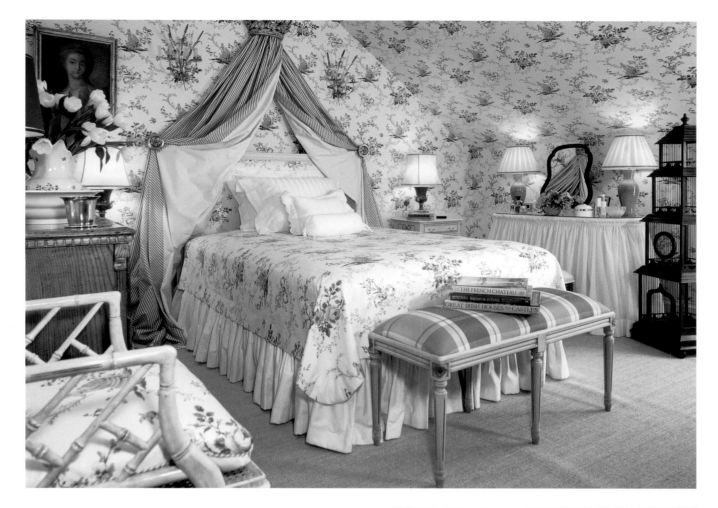

Wallpaper helps camouflage angled ceilings and other structural irregularities while adding coziness to country bedrooms. An old-fashioned dressing table and small writing desk invite lingering well into the morning. Design: Lise Davis Design at James Billings Antiques and Interiors
Photos: Peter Jaquith

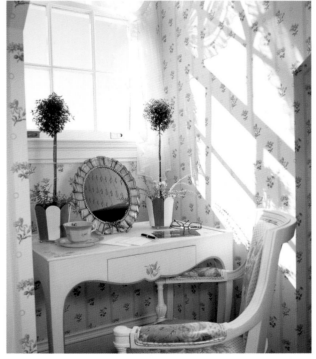

Use ribbons to tie the side panels of a grand manor canopy bed in various ways to create an open or closed nest as the mood strikes.
Design: Searl Design; Photo: Peter Paige

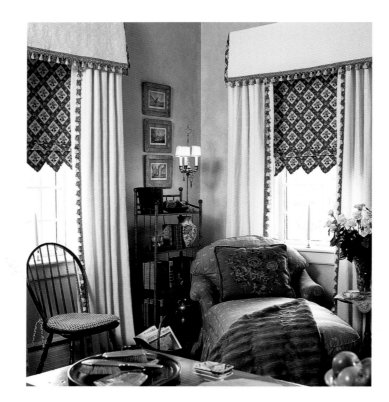

In a smaller bedroom where a canopy bed might
be too imposing, a draped treatment behind the
headboard creates a similar effect. The room's
design carefully coordinates details all the way
down to the Roman shades and floral pattern on
the ceiling. Design: Lillian Bogossian and Vivian
Weil, Decorative Interiors
Photos: Steve Vierra

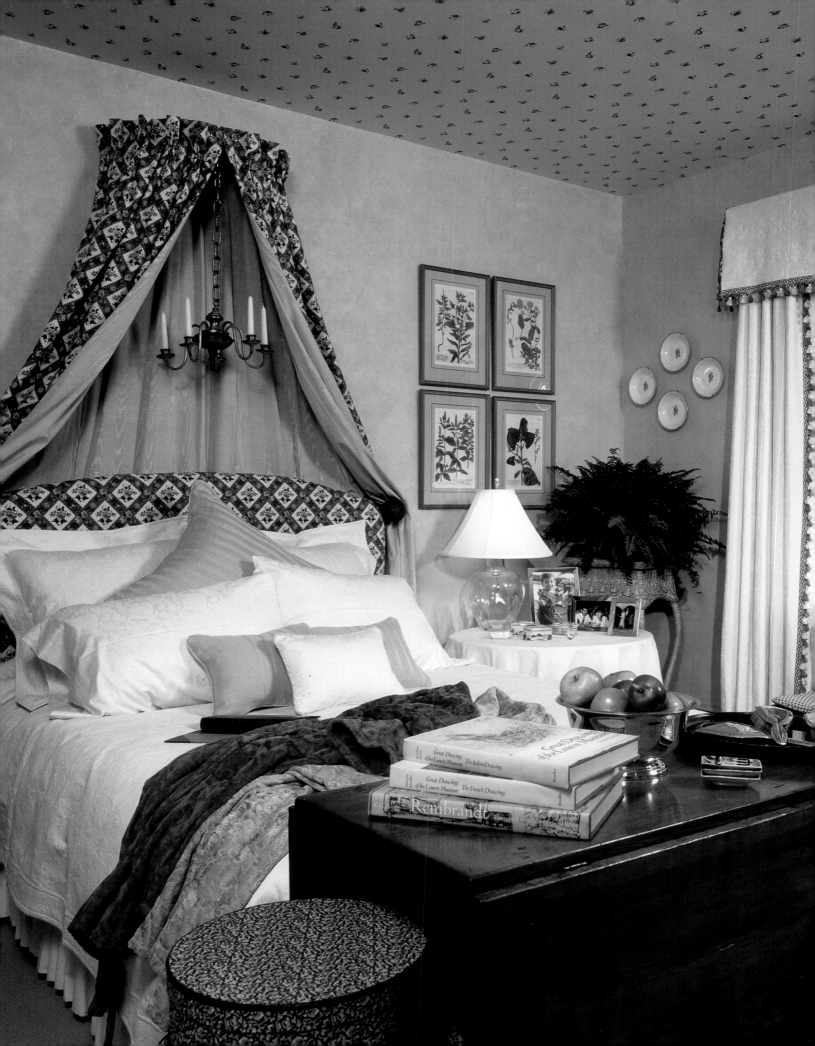

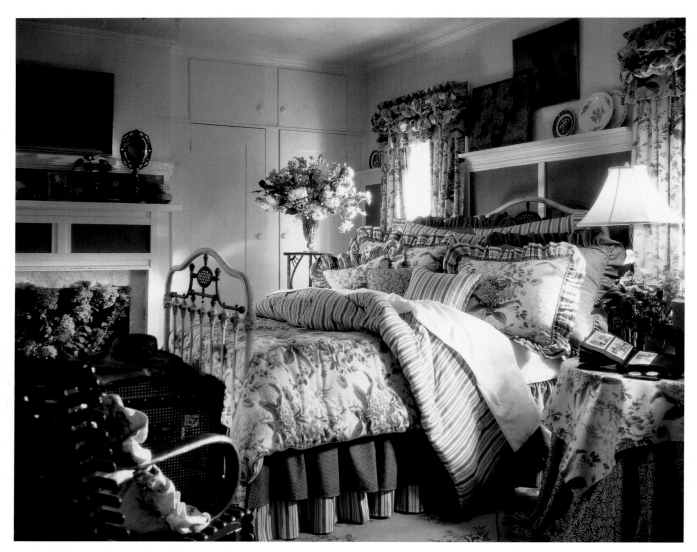

Layering fabrics, as in the tiered bed skirt and bedside tablecloths, creates a feminine look in romantic bedrooms. Photo courtesy of Waverly

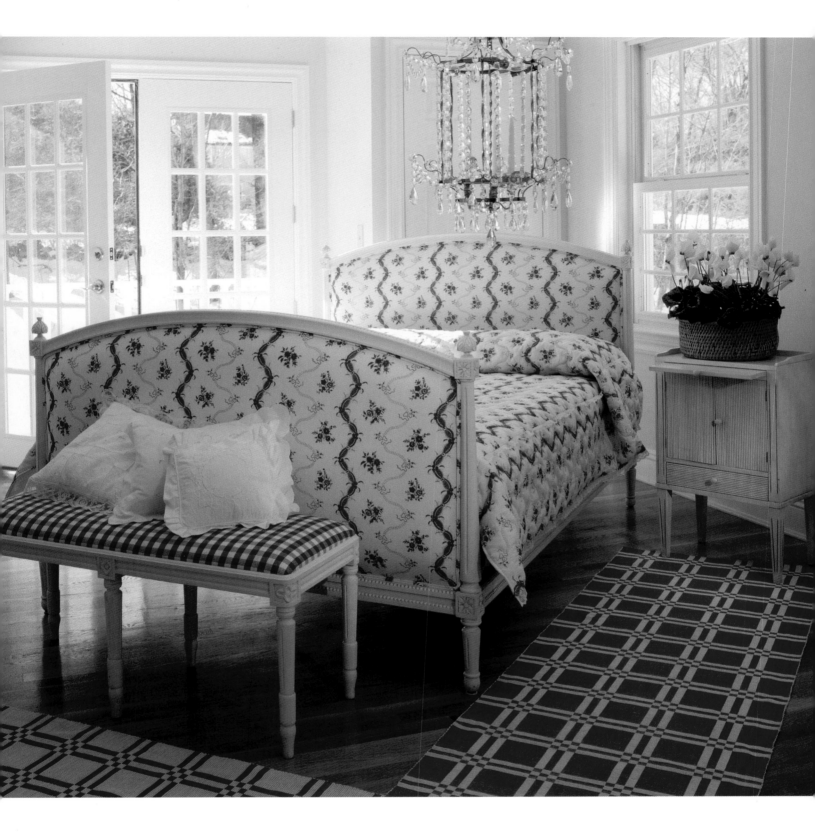

The painted furniture and crisp, clean patterns and colors typical of Swedish style combine to create a pristine look in country bedrooms.

Photo courtesy of Country Swedish

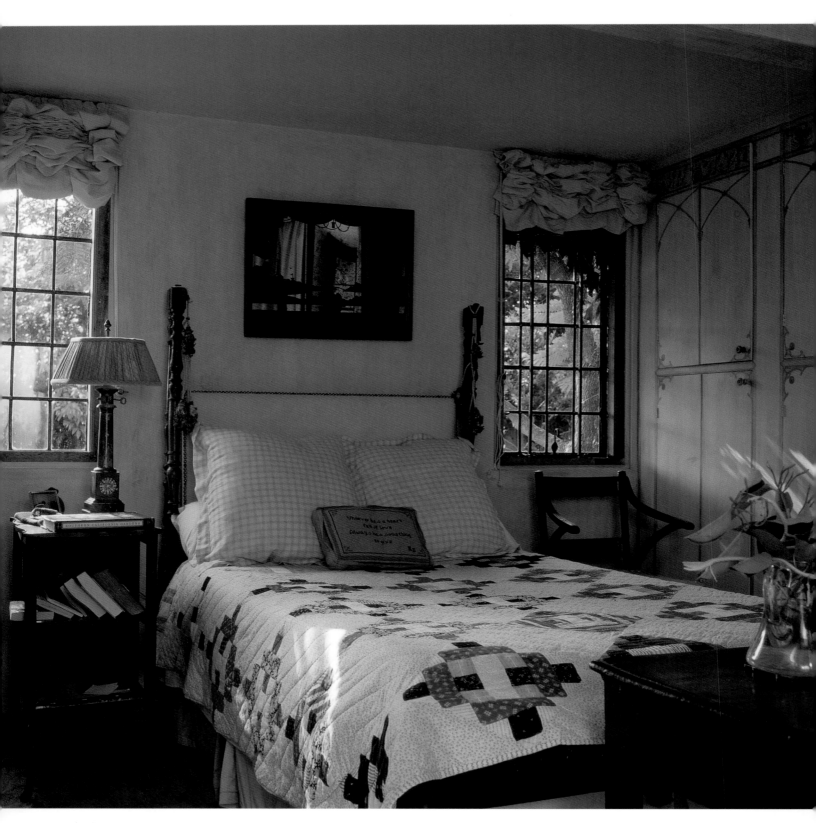

Decorative painting transforms the plain doors of built-in cabinets into one of this room's strongest features. Photo: Tim Street-Porter

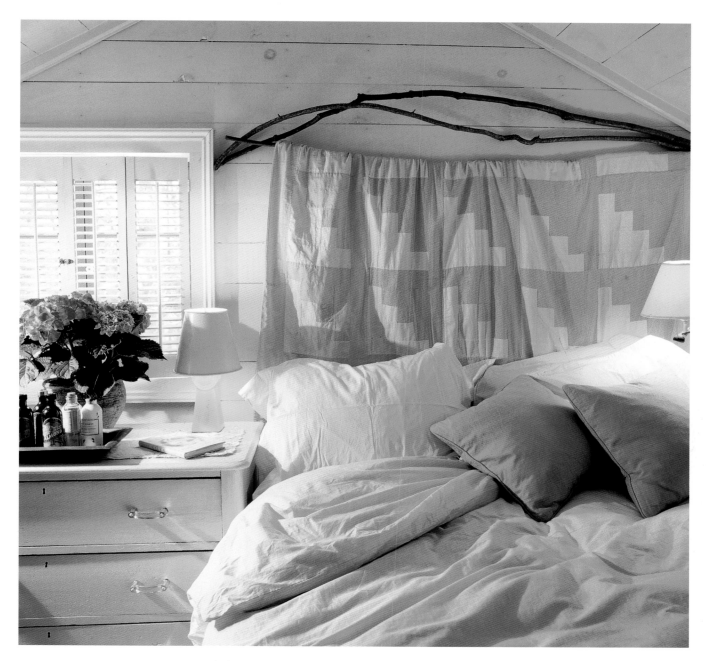

In this cottage bedroom tucked away beneath painted attic eaves, bare branches hold up a quilt "headboard" that keeps out drafts and adds pattern to the walls. Design: Cann & Company; Photo: Eric Roth

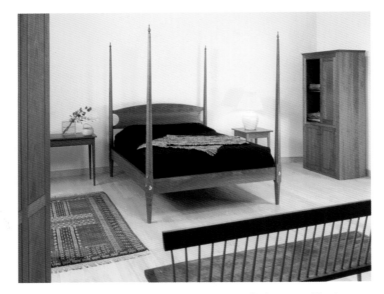

Simplicity is the byword in new country interiors. Here Shaker-inspired furniture and a cherry pencil-post bed are treated with minimalism reminiscent of meditative Japanese interiors. Photo: Paul Rocheleau, courtesy of Thos. Moser Cabinetmakers

Vividly colored bedspreads and other touche
red brighten and energize this rustic log cabi
retreat. Design: Allison Holland; Photo: Davi
Duncan Livingston

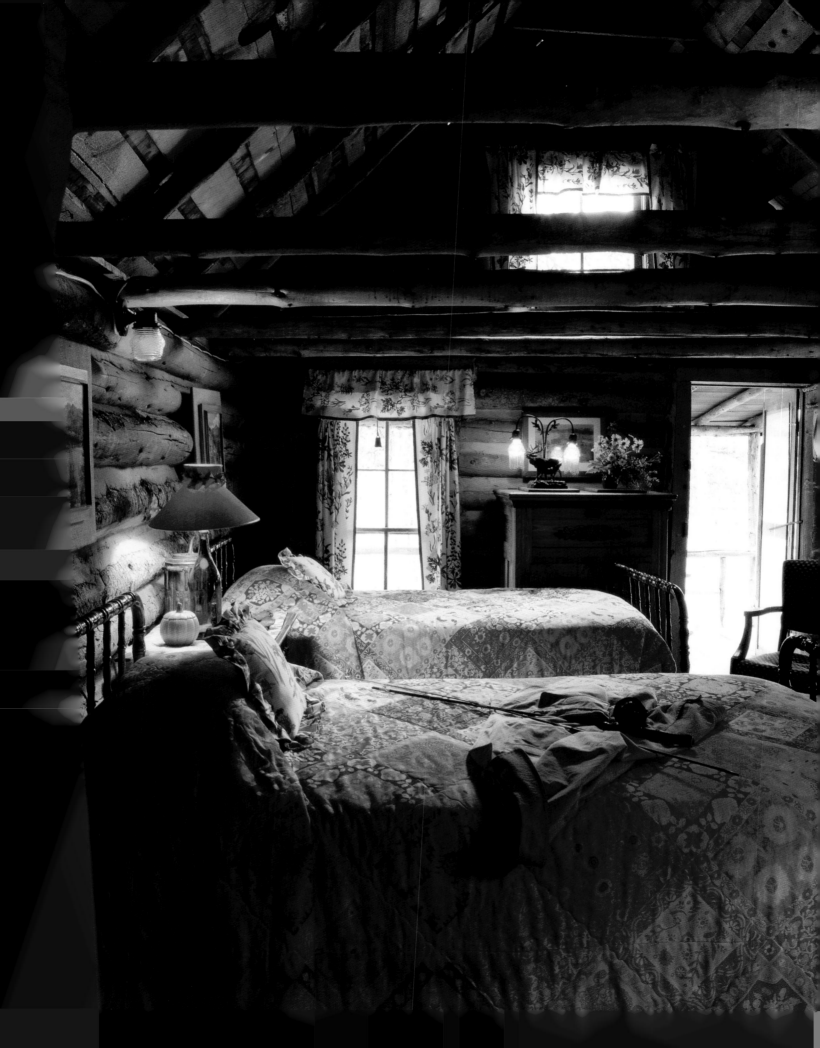

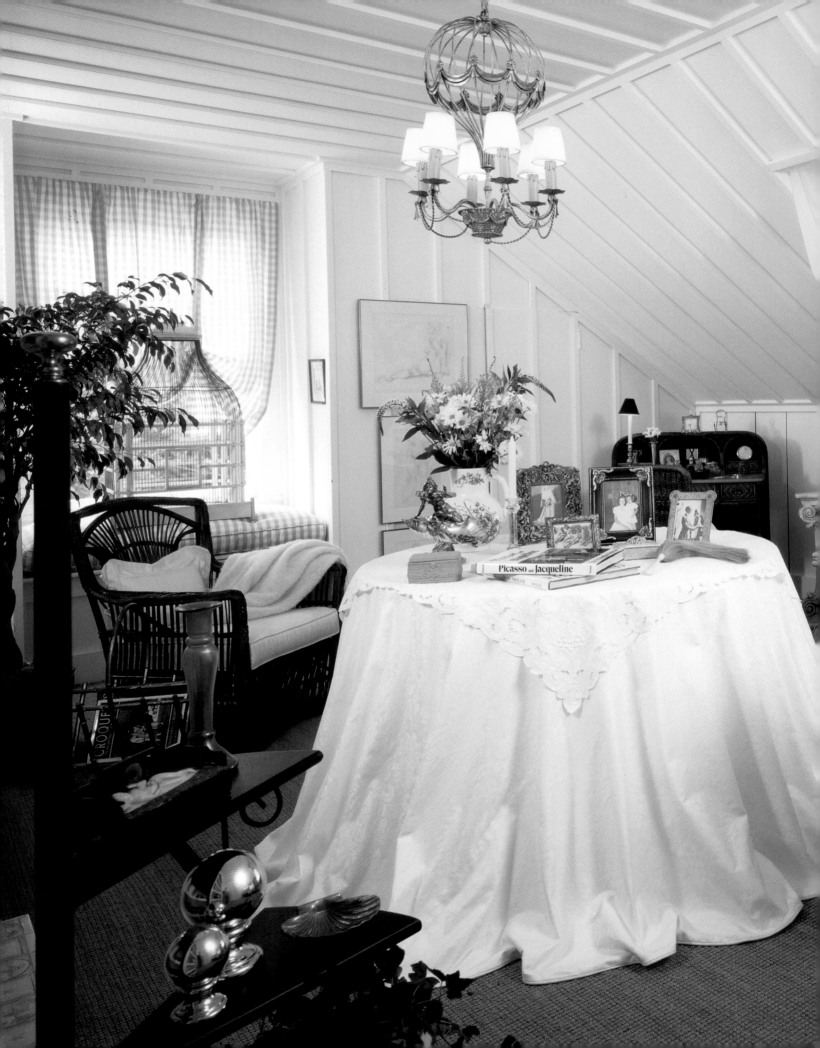

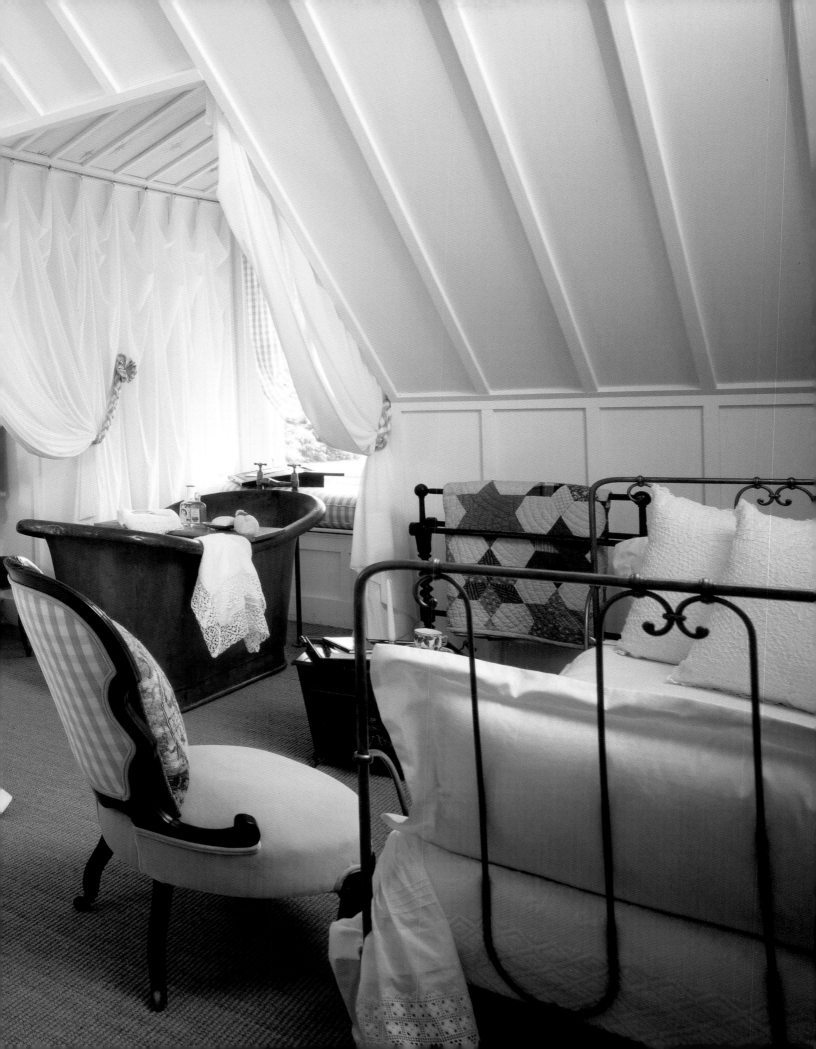

Previous pages: An ivory and taupe palette
emphasizes the room's dark elements: the wicker
furniture, antique bathtub, and whimsical gold
light suspended like a hot-air balloon in midflight.
Loosely draped muslin fabric softens the dormer
window. Design: Mary Rinaldi
Photo: Bill Rothschild

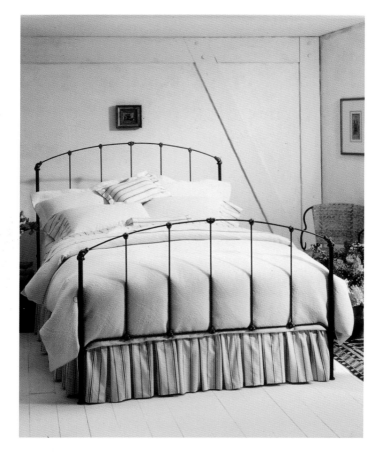

Exposed structural beams and support frames fit right in with the honesty and lack
of affectation at the heart of country style. In the best designs, though, comfort is
never sacrificed. This graceful iron bedstead is piled with soft pillows and
blankets. Photo courtesy of Charles P. Rogers Brass and Iron Beds

Checkered floors have long been a mainstay of
country kitchens, but bedrooms also benefit from
this time-tested design element. A subdued color
scheme of taupe and ivory ensures that the overall effect is calm and serene.
Photo courtesy of Charles P. Rogers Brass
and Iron Beds

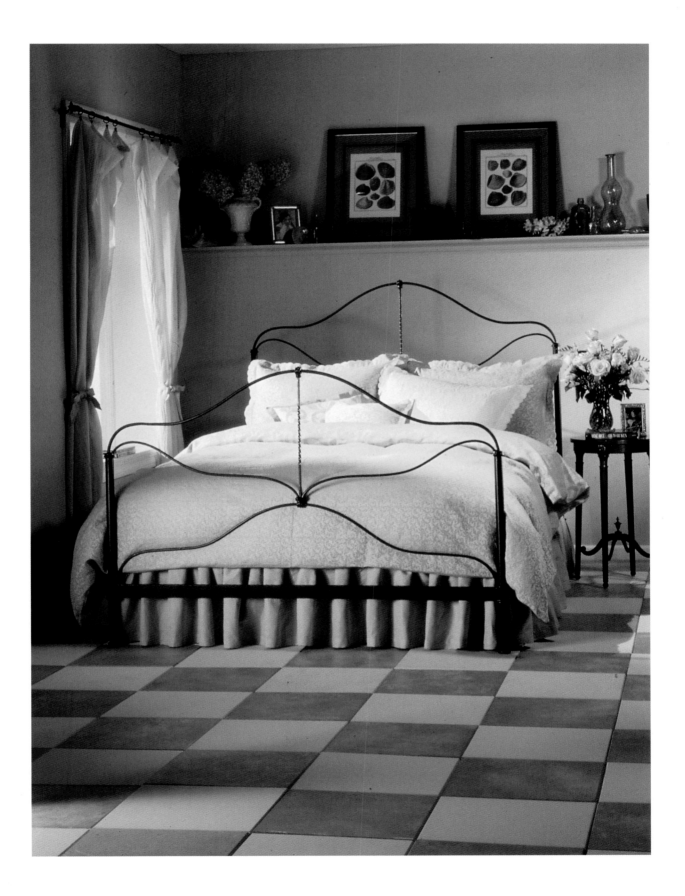

Piece by Piece *Bedroom* *details*

*When putting the pieces together in bedrooms, create a classic country look by piling plush pillows and comforters onto a brass or wrought-iron bedstead. Since bedrooms are for more than just sleeping, add desks, dressing tables, and chaises for versatility and style.*

*Keep It Simple*

The simple style of fabric window shades works beautifully in country bedrooms, with lace insets adding an elegant, handmade dimension. White wooden shutters, with their clean and linear look, afford privacy but let in varying amounts of light (below).

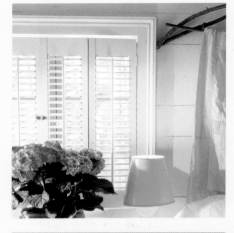

*Bedtime Stories*

Comfortable chaises longues and antique desks add a welcome dimension to bedrooms, whose intimate ambience is ideal for quiet activities such as reading and writing (below).
Top photo design: Austin Patterson Disston Architects; Photo: Fred George
Bottom photo: Furniture and fabrics by Summer Hill Ltd.

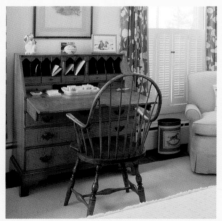

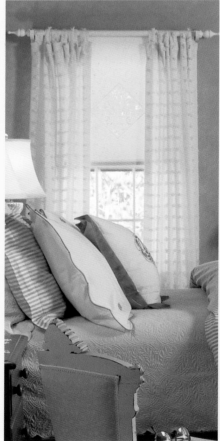

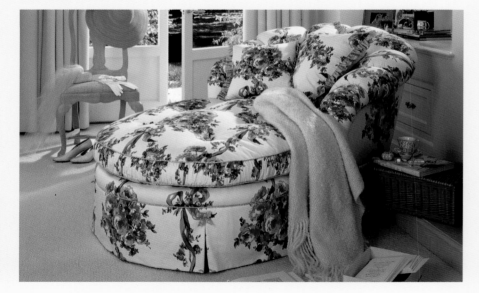

## Bedroom Storage

Armoires and simple built-in cabinetry hide away clothing, extra bed linens, and televisions. Also use decorated hatboxes, steamer trunks, and baskets to control bedroom clutter (below).

## Center Stage

In most bedrooms, the bedstead itself is the centerpiece. Brass and white wrought iron are perennial favorites for beds with floral linens, bed skirts, and thick comforters. More tailored alternatives include a painted and upholstered bed, popular in Swedish interiors (below).

Top photo courtesy of Charles P. Rogers Brass and Iron Beds
Center photo design: Eleanor E. Samuels, Abbott Interiors; Photo: Peter Jaquith
Bottom photo courtesy of Country Swedish

## Pattern on Pattern

When mixing checked, plaid, floral, and striped fabrics in country bedrooms, limit the palette to two or three colors for a serene look (below).
Photo courtesy of Brunschwig & Fils

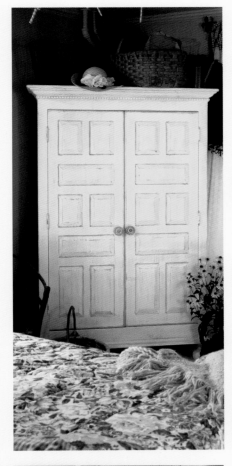

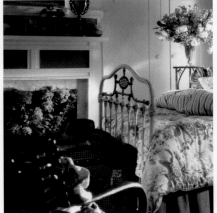

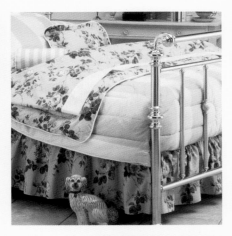

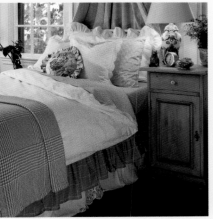

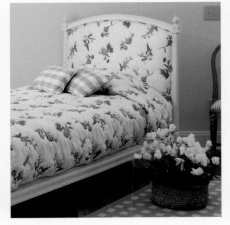

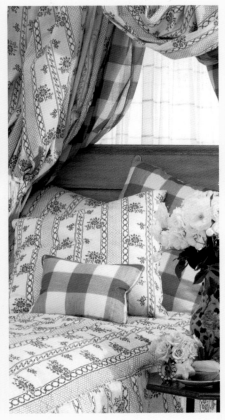

## Designers and Manufacturers

Eleanor E. Samuels
Abbott Interiors
169 Park Street
Newton, MA 02158

Susan Allen
1403 Evergreen Point Road
Medina, WA 98039

Anthony Antine
200 East 77th Street
New York, NY 10022

Anthony Catalfano Interiors Inc.
71 Newbury Street
Boston, MA 02116

Marisa Morra
Artistic and Historic Interiors
9 Jones Road
Weston, MA 02193

Lillian August
17 Main Street
Westport, CT 06880

Austin Patterson Disston Architects
376 Pequot Avenue
P.O. Box 61
Southport, CT 06490

David Barrett
131 East 71st Street
New York, NY 10021

Barbara Barry
9526 Pico Boulevard
Los Angeles, CA 90035

Chris Benson
Benson Interiors
411 Shawmut Avenue, Suite 4
Boston, MA 02118

Brunschwig & Fils
979 Third Avenue
New York, NY 10022

Cann & Company
450 Harrison Avenue
Boston, MA 02118

Charles P. Rogers Brass and
  Iron Beds
899 First Avenue
New York, NY 10022

Maggie Cohen
40 East 88th Street
New York, NY 10028

Constance Driscoll Design
  Consultants
13 Dartmouth Street
Boston, MA 02116

Constance Gallagher Interior Design
11 Adams Street
Charlestown, MA 02129

Neil Cooper
Cooper Pacific Kitchens, Inc.
Pacific Design Center
8687 Melrose Avenue, Suite G776
West Hollywood, CA 90069

Country Swedish
The D&D Building, Suite 1409
979 Third Avenue
New York, NY 10022

Crate and Barrel
For information and the nearest store,
call (800) 451-8217

Davis + Maltz Architects
270 Lafayette Street, Suite 307
New York, NY 10012

Lillian Bogossian and Vivian Weil
Decorative Interiors
162 Elm Street
Manchester Center, VT 05255

de Guilio kitchen design, inc.
1121 Central Avenue
Wilmette, IL 60091
674 North Wells Street
Chicago, IL 60610

Diane Hughes Interiors
Seacoast Village
29 Lafayette Road
North Hampton, NH 03862

Domain Home Fashions
For store locations, call
(800) 4-DOMAIN

Tony Duquette
1354 Dawnridge Drive
Beverly Hills, CA 90210

Elizabeth Klee Speert, Inc.
53 Barnard Avenue
Watertown, MA 02172

Faye Etter Interior Design
8 Varick Road
Waban, MA 02168

Susan Zises Green
11 East 44th Street
New York, NY 10017

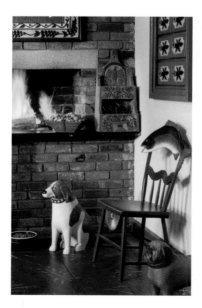

Gustavson/Dundes Architecture
and Design
192 Lexington Avenue, Suite 801
New York, NY 10016

Marlys Hann
52 West 84th Street
New York, NY 10024

Allison Holland
168 Poloke Place
Honolulu, HI 96822
6560 Long Peak Route
Estes Park, CO 80517

Stephen Huneck
RFD #1
St. Johnsbury, VT 05819

IKEA
For store locations, call
(410) 931–8940
or (626) 912–1119

Nancy Fowler and Cynthia Francis
Interior Design Concepts
7 Glen Oak Drive
Wayland, MA 01778

Kalman Construction
67 Milestone Road
Nantucket, MA 02554

Kay Bailey McKallagat Interiors
261 Main Street
West Newbury, MA 01985

Annie Kelly
2074 Watsonia Terrace
Los Angeles, CA 90068

Julie Vagts
The Kitchen Works
16 East Holly Street
Pasadena, CA 91103

Kohler Co.
444 Highland Drive
Kohler, WI 53044

Lester Korzilius, Architect
3 Riverside
22 Hester Road
London Sw11 4AN, UK

Martin Kuckly
506 East 74th Street
New York, NY 10021

Jeanne Leonard
19 Mitchell Street
Westhampton Beach, NY 11978

Lise Davis Design at James Billings
Antiques and Interiors
34 Charles Street
Boston, MA 02114

Diane Chase Madden
P.O. Box 729
Sandwich, MA 02563

Mark Hutker & Associates
P.O. Box 2347
Vineyard Haven, MA 02566

Gary McBournie Inc.
33A North Main Street
Sherborn, MA 01770

Milling Road
A Division of Baker Furniture
329 North Hamilton Street
High Point, NC 27260

Manijeh M. Emery
M. M. Interiors
P.O. Box 160
Osterville, MA 02655

Brett Nestler
350 East 79th Street
New York, NY 10021

New West
2811 Big Horn Avenue
Cody, WY 82414
Paris Ceramics
151 Greenwich Avenue
Greenwich, CT 06830

Kevin and Joanne Paulsen
P.O. Box 2838
Nantucket, MA 02584

Judy Collins and Bob Collins
Peach Tree Designs
173 Main Street
Yarmouth Port, MA 02675

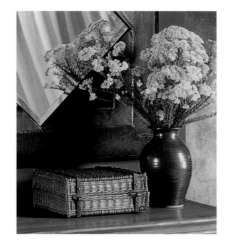

Phyllis D. Green Interiors
50 Mill Road
Ipswich, MA 01938

Pierre Deux
404 Airport Executive Park
Nanuet, NY 10954

Nancy Goslee Power
1660 Stanford Street
Santa Monica, CA 90404

Mary Rinaldi
142 Jessup Avenue
Quogue, NY 11959

Robert Clark + Raymond LeCuyer
333 West 57th Street
New York, NY 10019

Van Martin Rowe
195 South Parkwood Avenue
Pasadena, CA 91107

Joe Ruggiero
4512 Louise Street
Encino, CA 91316

Alexis Ryan
28 Manor Road
Huntington, NY 11743

Sandra J. Bissell Interior Design
337 Summer Street
North Andover, MA 01845

Searl Design
808 Garnet Circle
Fort Lauderdale, FL 33326

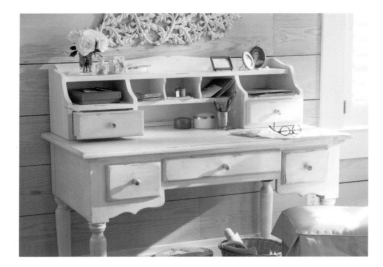

Teri Seidman
150 East 61st Street
New York, NY 10021

SieMatic
886 Town Center Drive
Langhorne, PA 19047

Sue Adams Interiors
110 Haggetts Pond Road
Andover, MA 01810

Summer Hill Ltd.
2682h Middlefield Road
Redwood City, CA 94063

Thomson Architects
884 West End Avenue
New York, NY 10025

Thos. Moser Cabinetmakers
72 Wright's Landing
P.O. Box 1237
Auburn, ME 04211

Jody Trail and Susan Maier
Trail-Maier Design
68 Windsor Road
Sudbury, MA 01776

Leslie Fetherston Tuttle
Tuttle-Bradley
315 Essex Street
Salem, MA 01970

Waterworks
29 Park Avenue
Danbury, CT 06810

Waverly
A Division of F. Scumacher & Co.
79 Madison Avenue
New York, NY 10016

Weatherend Estate Furniture
Imagineering, Inc.
6 Gordon Drive
Rockland, MA 04841

Carole Harmon
White House Farm
69 Foster Centre Road
Foster, RI 02825

Wood-Mode Inc.
1 Second Street
Kreamer, PA 17833

## Photographers

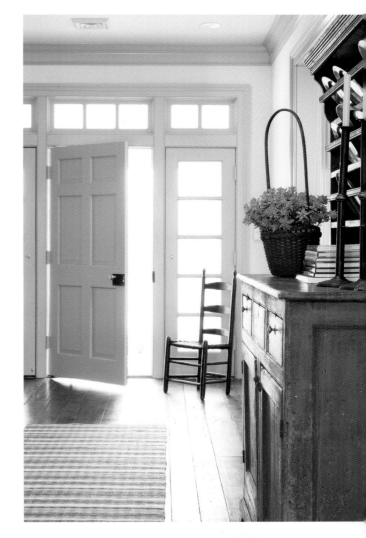

Jean Allsopp
1504 Grove Place
Birmingham, AL 35209

Robert Benson
140 Huyshope Avenue
Hartford, CT 06146

Jeff Guerrant
1945 Techny Road, #5
Northbrook, IL 60062

Peter Jaquith
6 Pleasant Street
Beverly, MA 01915

Balthazar Korab
P.O. Box 895
Troy, MI 48099

David Duncan Livingston
1036 Erica Road
Mill Valley, CA 94941
www.davidduncanlivingston.com

Ron Maier
2538 Cowgill Road
Cody, WY 82414

Jeff McNamara
68 Vista
Easton, CT 06612

Peter Paige
269 Parkside Road
Harrington Park, NJ 07640

Kenton Robertson
4004-M Spring Garden Street
Greensboro, NC 27407

Paul Rocheleau
482 Canaan Road
Richmond, MA 01254

Eric Roth
337 Summer Street
Boston, MA 02210

Bill Rothschild
19 Judith Lane
Wesley Hills, NY 10952

Mikio Sekita
79 Leonard Street
New York, NY 10013

Tim Street-Porter
2074 Watsonia Terrace
Los Angeles, CA 90068

Steve Vierra
P.O. Box 1827
Sandwich, MA 02563

Paul Warchol
133 Mulberry Street
New York, NY 10013

Wade Zimmerman
9 East 97th Street
New York, NY 10029

Carol Meredith writes about interior design and architecture for magazines, newspapers, and professional design firms. During her fifteen years in the field, she has served as managing editor for *Texas Homes* magazine, and home and garden editor for *New England Living*. Her articles have also appeared in *Design Times*, *Boston* magazine, and the *Boston Globe*. She is author of the recent book, *Eclectic Style in Interior Design*. Ms. Meredith lives in New Hampshire with her husband, David Reynolds, and stepdaughters Anne and Aleisha.